Carry on Regardless

Robin Page

Illustrated by John Paley

BIRD'S FARM BOOKS

By the Same Author
The Benefits Racket
Down Among the Dossers
The Decline of an English Village
The Hunter and the Hunted
Weather-forecasting the Country Way
Cures and Remedies the Country Way
Animal Cures the Country Way
Weeds the Country Way
The Journal of a Country Parish
Journeys into Britain
The Country Ways of Love
The Wildlife of the Royal Estates
A Fox's Tale
The Fox and the Orchid
Dust in a Dark Continent (Africa)
Gardening the Country Way
A Peasant's Diary
Gone to the Dogs
Vocal Yokel
Carry on Farming
The Hunting Gene
One Man Went to Mow
The Great British Butterfly Safari

Children's Books
How the Fox got its Pointed Nose
How the Heron got Long Legs
Why the Rabbit Stamps its Foot
How the Hedgehog got its Prickles
Why the Reindeer has a Velvet Nose

Published by Bird's Farm Books, Barton, Cambridgeshire CB3 7AG
Distributed by Bird's Farm Books

Reprinted 2006

Reprinted 2007

ISBN 0 905232 25 9

Designed by Jim Reader

Printed and bound in Great Britain by Nightingale Press,
Royston, Hertfordshire

Carry on Regardless

DEDICATION

*I am dedicating this book with all my love
to my lovely wife 'Lulu', Anita or even Mrs Page.*

*Also to all friends of the real countryside
and to vocal yokels everywhere.*

© ANDREW CROWLEY, THE DAILY TELEGRAPH

Robin Page is a farmer, writer, conservationist and publisher – he is a vocal yokel. He tries to practice what he preaches through his farm and The Countryside Restoration Trust, of which he is Chairman. He has stood for Parliament almost as many times as he has been arrested, but he does not regard himself as a politician – a species he views in the same way as magpies, slugs and assorted parasites. He lives with his wife Lulu on the farm where he was born and is addicted to village cricket and travelling off the beaten track in Africa and Britain.

Contents

Preface from a Vocal Yokel

Much has happened since my last book on the general countryside – *One Man Went to Mow*. Those people living and working in rural Britain have had to put up with a lot in five years: foot-and-mouth: Mad Cow Disease: Mrs Beckett: supermarkets: bureaucracy: Tony Blair: European Directives: bird flu: prejudice: thought control: Prescott: Looney development: the CAP: ignorant urban MPs: manic officials: Political Correctness: soya sucking vegetarians: the Cuddly Bunny Syndrome: discrimination: regulation: intimidation, these are the things attacking the countryside and rural culture in a so-called 'multi-cultural society'. Oh dear, what shall we do? Give up? Certainly not, there is only one thing to be done – CARRY ON REGARDLESS.

Fortunately I am not the only one proud of Britain's rural inheritance – and *Carry on Regardless* simply shows how real life continues despite the aggravation and interference from the government and its assorted quangoes and jobworths – the modern day Quislings. Sleepwalking Britons have allowed Blair and his cronies to heap regulation, legislation and restriction, on a people once proud to be considered democratic and free. They have seen agriculture almost brought to its knees; rural communities ruined and hunting banned. Never mind, we will CARRY ON REGARDLESS.

In the process of defending the countryside I have even been put into a police cell – quite illegally – for calling on country people to be given the same freedoms as other minority groups. Two members of the Gloucestershire Constabulary came all the way to Cambridge and arrested me because they had received 'a complaint'. No law had been broken of course, but Mr Plod explained that I could be guilty of 'incitement'. I find virtually every utterance from our modern MPs an incitement, but nobody arrests them. Bomber Blair broke the law during foot and mouth, yet nobody has arrested him. It seems that the Concrete King of Britain, John Prescott, broke the law of incitement during the election of 2005 – oh, surprise, surprise, nobody arrested him either. 'The rule of law'? Sorry – in Britain it is now the manipulation of the law – never mind, there is only one thing to be done – CARRY ON REGARDLESS.

I would like to thank John Paley for his excellent cover and cartoons; Jim Reader for his design; Jemma Hooper for trying to cope with my writing idiosyncrasies and the Nightingale Press in Royston (Carol and Peter Matthews) for printing *Carry On Regardless*.

I would like to thank the Editors of *The Daily Telegraph*, *The Countryman*, *The Daily Mail*, *The Mail on Sunday* and *The Shooting Times* for allowing me to reproduce articles appearing here. There is one slight difference however – on this occasion they are all unexpurgated – in other words even more politically incorrect than usual – who cares – we should all CARRY ON REGARDLESS.

1

The Decline of an English Village

———

I am an oddity, or even a rarity, in Blair's high-tech, 21st Century Britain – I still live next door to the house where I was born; on the farm where my father worked for sixty years; in the village where I went to school and in the parish where I collected tadpoles and found a new-born fox cub which became a pet. It was an idyllic childhood; the pace of life was as it had been for generations; two cart horses stood side by side in the stable and each day during the summer the Dairy Shorthorn cows walked from the farm to the fields and then back again for milking. The few cars didn't just slow, they stopped, as the main road through the village was not wide enough for a string of cows and old Ford cars. From the cows we had fresh milk, unpasteurised, every day, and sometimes my mother made butter. When a cow calved we had 'bisnings' – a delicious pudding made from the thick fresh milk of a newly calved cow – the curds and whey of Little Miss Muffet – now considered to be a health hazard, but which we loved and it did us no harm.

We walked over half a mile from the farm to the school every weekday, walking under larksong, looking at wild-flowers, finding birds' nests and being sent to stand in the corner for being late. We were in the corner again for playing kiss chase during playtime, but we considered it to be a punishment well worth the crime. On a hot summer afternoon Miss Whitmell, our teacher, would close her

books and put away her chalk: 'Let's go for a nature walk'
– at the village pond we looked for newts; along the drift we
heard the 'Little bit of bread and no cheese' of the
yellowhammer and again there was the spiralling chorus of
the larks.

On the farm we were lucky to have parents who loved
their life. They were excited by each new calf; they worked
hard during sowing and gave thanks at the chapel's harvest
festival when the corn had been safely gathered in. But
their pleasure was not just limited to the farm crops and
animals; they were excited by the first call of the cuckoo in the
spring; they welcomed the swallows that nested in the garage
and they loved the wild harvest of late summer – blackberries,
mushrooms and crab apples for crab apple jam. It was a life
in which farming and nature were in harmony and the whole
village appreciated the land and the seasons of the year that
produced food and gave them pleasure.

How it has changed – possibly as fast as at any time in
recorded history. The animals have gone from nearly all the
fields and as I speak huge combine harvesters prowl the
prairie fields in clouds of their own dust. No cattle dare walk
the widened roads as juggernauts bear down at frightening
speeds and few unaccompanied children are allowed to walk
to school. Yes, the village school still stands in the heart of
the village but the children are locked in during class time for
their own safety. The village bobby on a bike has been
replaced by a panda car, which in turn has become as rare as
the call of the cuckoo – crime is almost out of control and
nobody with their brain cells working dare leave the doors
and windows of their houses open or even unlocked.
Incredibly even the parish pump (a listed building) has
been stolen and a holly tree in the churchyard was cut down
and taken away in about three minutes, just before one
Christmas.

At night the glare of streetlights hides the stars and there is constant moving light as planes circle the sky for Stansted and for Luton. The countryside has become a factory farm; villages have become dormitories and communities have been torn apart. Old houses have been 'tarted up'; new houses have been built in old meadows and even the vicar has left the vicarage, which has been sold off by the Diocese of Ely to a property developer. In a battle between God and Mammon, Mammon appears to have won with the active help of the Church of England. Of my old friends in the village school, few still live in the village – they cannot afford the fancy prices. The tarting-up process has almost been completed with the arrival of goldfish in the village pond.

Sadly, the story of my village is not unusual, as the same sequence of events has hit most of the rural parishes throughout the country. Change had to come and some change can be beneficial. But rural change has, in the main, been ill-considered change being driven by greed, big business and political and environmental ignorance. 'Progress' and an increase in the standard of living has been the political aim, totally divorced from 'quality of life' – and so as the countryside has become richer, the quality of life has become poorer. Increased development has given new housing estates, intrusive roads, traffic queues, idiotic airports, light pollution, noise pollution, air pollution and stress. At the same time wildlife has been obliterated by the industrialisation of agriculture and suburbia's obsession with tidiness. Milk lakes and wheat mountains have been more important than skylarks and the brown hare, and the shining BMW in the garage has been considered far more valuable than the nesting swallows. Those who have been driving this development, and the attitudes that go with it, have not realised that communities have grown over hundreds of years for reasons of geography, geology, travel and trade and that a community is an organism that needs care, continuity and understanding.

Care, continuity and understanding for the countryside is something totally unknown to this countryside illiterate Labour Government and having John Prescott in charge of countryside planning is like having the fox in charge of the henhouse. In fact John Prescott is to 'sustainable communities' what Mike Tyson is to flower arranging. In my small area of Cambridgeshire, Prescott is ordering a wave of 40,000 new houses – an entirely phoney building boom, which he is extending to the whole of southern Britain, although the need is based on doubtful logic and flawed economics. The whole area is already more densely populated than India and China and there is not enough water to service the development – in other words his mind-set is Third World, yet John Prescott clearly sees himself as the Concrete King of Southern England.

At the same time this despicable Labour Government, under the guise of local government reform, has stripped away the planning responsibilities from local councils, thus removing the voice of rural communities. Instead, power has been given to Prescott's quislings, to the unelected, undemocratic Regional Assemblies – the playthings of the European super-state. Yes, it would seem that New Labour wants democracy in Iraq, but not in rural Britain; perhaps 'Two Jags' should really be called Osama Bin Prescott.

Over thirty years ago I saw the warning signs of the impending rural disaster when I wrote *The Decline of an English Village*. It was written as a warning – trying to alert those who rule us about the dangers to the countryside, to our village communities and to our wildlife. It went largely unheeded. Indeed since then I have written hundreds of thousands, possibly millions of words about the rural disaster. The pen mightier than the sword? I don't think so.

After thirty years of the Common Agricultural Policy we have twelve farms going out of business every day; with one farming suicide every six days, and the supermarkets are having a field day as the free market in food has become a supermarket monopoly. Of course, in 2002 Tony Blair, well known for his fantasies, vowed to break the 'armlock' of the supermarkets. Instead he made the supermarket supplier and apologist Lord Haskins his farming guru. Prescott's answer is even simpler; he does not see land in terms of communities and food production but in terms of 'development'. His pet phrase to hide his environmental illiteracy is 'sustainable communities'; he seems incapable of realising that communities cannot be built or that his development is environmentally unsustainable. Indeed the main driving force for his development – strange in a so-called socialist – is money.

The last thirty years have been astonishing. The M11 motorway was bulldozed through the northern part of my parish – sold locally as 'the Cambridge Western Bypass', whereas in reality it always was the major link road that would make Stansted possible. Dutch elm disease has taken away our most dominant and beautiful hedgerow tree; this controllable disease only became uncontrollable as local authorities spent time arguing over who was responsible for control, instead of getting on with the job. The CAP has devastated our wildlife – giving subsidies for production, rather than the methods of production; and as a consequence hedges have been ripped out, wetlands have been drained and wildlife has been hammered almost into oblivion. The whole philosophy of 'mobility of labour' has been another nail in the coffin of rural communities. With new houses have come new accents – from Yorkshire, Liverpool, Scotland and Wales – many belonging to people who do not understand village or farming life. What was wanted was 'stability of labour' – jobs to people where they were needed, rather than people to jobs – so during the high tech revolution we are making exactly the same social and environmental mistakes that were made during the industrial revolution.

In thirty years, too many of the old skills and characters have also gone, not to be replaced. My old father could lay a hedge and calve a cow; Bert ran the local shop and sold English plums and marrows almost too big to carry and Charlie, the only man to limp while riding a bike, would tell a great variety of stories, both true and blue, as we stacked the bales. There were so many characters and incidents – the old ditcher who went to the doctor's wanting a sick note. 'What's wrong?' The doctor asked him. 'I can only lift my arm up to here', he said slowly raising his left hand up to his chest.

'And how far can you usually raise it?'

'Right up to here', he replied stretching his arm and hand well above his head.

There were men who could charm warts, graft trees, thatch roofs, forecast the weather and poach a pheasant. There was more to wildlife than pheasants – there were hares running in their March madness; my pet fox that escaped, only to come back to eat the hens; a kestrel whose wing was mended with sticky brown paper and the cockerel with a broken leg that my father set with plaster of Paris. It was only after the cast was off that he realised he had set the foot the wrong way round – the poor bird had no idea whether he was coming or going.

When he died my father was buried in the base of one of the farm hedges – his coffin carried by horse and cart. Sadly, as the old characters have gone, their replacements seem few and far between. 'Dormitory' seems blander than 'community'; 'factory farm' seems emptier than 'living countryside' and 'standard of living' seems less valuable than 'quality of life'.

But all is not lost. Seeing the wildlife disaster going on around me I joined with friends, including the artist the late Gordon Beningfield and Laurens van der Post, to form the Countryside Restoration Trust. From no members, no money and no land, we now have over 1,000 acres in Cambridgeshire, Herefordshire, Surrey and Yorkshire. At our Lark Rise Farm in my own parish, we are showing farmers how to farm with nature – not telling them. With grass margins, hay meadows, new hedges, smaller fields and abundant common sense we have seen our local wildlife flood back – otters, skylarks, yellowhammers, cowslips – and, after a break of over forty years, barn owls have bred successfully for the last five years. Even the mighty RSPB has followed our example by becoming involved with practical farming and there are elements of our success in the government's agricultural reforms – better late than never I suppose.

Still more can be done; the encouragement of farmers' markets and farmers' supermarkets could break the hold of the supermarkets and encourage people to buy quality food rather than cheap food, and seasonal and regional food rather than junk food. Then of course there is a way of defeating John Prescott and his undemocratic Regional Assemblies – it is known as democracy and the ballot box. Yes, and there should be building too – new factories in the areas where work is needed – continuity of labour not mobility of labour. It would all be so simple if only our politicians had the vision to match their egos.

2

Father MacChristmas and his Scottish Reindeer

Not a lot of people know this – but at the moment there is a serial criminal criss-crossing Britain. No, it is not Tony Blair (well, he is not the serial criminal I have in mind), it is Father Christmas – or at least a whole gaggle of Father Christmases, each with his own group of beautiful reindeer. The laws they break are so numerous that I can hardly mention them all. They are paid well below the national minimum wage – indeed some of them are paid nothing; they are clearly guilty of impersonation as in real life there can only be one Father Christmas, and in addition Father Christmas outfits are so hot and sweaty that they must break several health, safety and hygiene rules. It can only be a matter of time before the

Brussels 'Santa Claus Directive' bypasses the House of Commons, as usual, and empties almost every over-heated grotto in Britain from Harrods to Hartlepool. Only last year I had the experience of being a 'ho ho basement Father Christmas' at a party in a fashionable London shop – together with a Mother Christmas. I have never been so hot in my life and it had nothing to do with the company or the gorgeous young ladies I had to bounce on my knees as part of the job.

No, in Blair's Britain the only genuine thing about Father Christmas is his reindeer, and even they no longer fly. The skies are so busy and overcrowded, thanks to Easy-Jet and Ryanair, that to avoid stacking over Luton, or the hazards of fog, Santa's friends travel from grotto to shopping centre by luxury lorry – making Rudolph's rednose totally redundant. They seem to thoroughly enjoy the lorry experience – returning to their vehicle almost as enthusiastically as the average car travelling dog. Now here lies the problem: the reindeer are doing so well that Tilly and Alan Smith of the Cairngorm reindeer herd – Britain's only herd of semi-domestic reindeer – actually need some more reindeer to introduce new blood-lines into their wonderful British herd.

The reindeer might secretly still want to fly, but I hate flying and with each new air-ticket my neurosis gets worse. It got worse in the summer when Tilly and Alan phoned me and said: 'We've got a job for you. Will you help Father Christmas and come up to Lapland with us?' No, wrong, it had nothing to do with Lap-dancing, and no, I was not wanted to audition as a Christmas elf. No, Tilly and Alan Smith, acting for Father MacChristmas, wanted to see some potential new reindeer for their herd, and they wanted to see them with the indigenous reindeer herders of Northern Sweden. What those traditional herders are correctly called I have no idea; just as 'Red Indians' have become 'Native Americans', 'Eskimos' have become 'Innuit', so 'Laplanders' are said to have become

'Saami' 'Sami' or 'Shami', depending on who you talk to. Unusually some of the Saami themselves are evidently talking to the wrong people as they still refer to themselves as 'Lapps'. Odd that – a cultural minority being politically incorrect about themselves. They are not the only ones suffering from political incorrectness, for way up in their summer pastures, well into the Arctic Circle, birdwatchers are still watching 'Lapland buntings' – not yet designated Saamiland buntings by the PC thought-police.

It does feel strange driving a thousand miles north from Stockholm through to the Saami summer settlement of Vaisaluokta overlooking Lake Akkajaure – one of Sweden's 260,000 lakes. What a pleasure – in the whole round trip we only saw three abandoned cars and one discarded beer can. On a recent journey from Cambridge to Ipswich I counted eight abandoned cars – some of them burnt out – and saw enough litter to fill three dustcarts; Britain must have become the litter and filth capital of Europe.

For lovers of midges and mosquitoes, in uncountable millions, 'The Land of the Midnight Sun' is wonderful. The snow-capped mountains of the Sarek National Park, forests, lakes, wildlife and reindeer under 24 hours of continuous sunlight are spectacular. The birds of a Lapland summer are fascinating – fieldfares, redwings and waxwings, the birds of an English winter, and the breeding swallows and calling cuckoos above the Arctic circle seem to be doing far better than in my part of East Anglia.

The Saami were welcoming and generous. One foolish herdsman tried to out-drink a Scotman; he lost, and Alan went for a hill-run the next day as normal – trying to outrun the mosquitoes. Herding the reindeer for the annual 'calf marking' started at midnight – the cool of the day. In a recent BBC programme 'Running with Reindeer' the viewers were informed 'the Saami are leading the same life that they have led for a thousand years'. Amazing that, the 2,000 reindeer, and their 1,000 calves that I saw were rounded up by helicopters, scramble-motorbikes and All-Terrain Vehicles; the Saami themselves were wearing jeans and baseball caps, presumably to a 1,000-year-old design. Every herder has his own mark, which is cut into the ear of each calf, with a razor sharp knife.

The mark that Alan and Tilly wanted to see was that of the Utsi family – as the founder of the Cairngorm reindeer herd, the late Mikel Utsi, still has nephews and a brother herding reindeer in northern Sweden. The bulls were magnificent (not 'stags', BBC) with huge antlers in velvet. Several newcomers were chosen and now as Lapland slowly becomes 'The Land of the Mid-Day Moon' the soon to be Scottish reindeer are in quarantine. In the spring they will travel by lorry, boat or even plane to Scotland and next year at this time they too may be giving pleasure to thousands of children as they travel with assorted Father Christmases throughout Britain. Long live Father MacChristmas and his Scottish reindeer.

3

Here Comes the Bride – and the Heating Allowance

Suddenly life has changed; at the age of 61, with the heating allowance safely banked, I have got married for the very first time. In a matter of half a year I have experienced a change of life from being 'an unclaimed treasure' to becoming a re-constructed bachelor. What I have gained is a pretty wife from the next village – two miles as the crow flies, or the bicycle is pedalled – three stepchildren, three dogs, four cats, eight hens (declining steadily thanks to the activities of Reynard), two rather bored goldfish and one geriatric pony, also in need of a heating allowance. What Anita has lost is her widow's allowance.

The locals greeted the news with astonishment. All I heard was 'Robin she's gorgeous'; 'How did you do it?', and of course 'You don't know how lucky you are'. What Anita heard was completely different: 'Are you bonkers?' 'Have you seen the state of his house?'; 'How are you going to start – by having a jumble sale?'

There were others of course who were just bemused: 'What on earth do you want to get married for in this day and age?' To one I replied: 'Well at my time of life you need something warm in bed to ward off the cold during winter'. He was not impressed. 'In that case why didn't you get a good terrier?' he asked. 'That's simple', I replied, 'I've not yet found a terrier that can work the Hoover.' It may have been politically incorrect, but at least it made Anita laugh.

Another friend was even worse: 'I hope she's getting married in white', he said. 'Why?' I asked, puzzled. 'Well you want the dishwasher to match the freezer and the cooker don't you?' No, Anita was not getting married in white. 'Oh well', he sighed, 'make sure she's got small feet – it will enable her to stand nearer to the sink.'

The reason we decided to get married was that we wanted to. Yes, even in this cynical day and age we fell in love. I met her briefly at a nearby point-to-point meeting, and then friends asked me to contact her again on a local issue. I must have received strange but romantic subliminal messages from their names – thank you Pat and Roger. I phoned, we chatted, we met again; in four months we were engaged and in seven months – married.

When the day dawned I was in a state of mild hysteria. It was Anita who had decided that we should marry on the shortest day, as I only have a bath on the longest day and the shortest. I was wheezing like one of my old sheep and for the first time in months grabbed my inhaler. I was feeling nervous and nauseous. I took two soluble aspirins and put some whisky in my coffee – it made no difference. I had never felt like this before and it couldn't be morning sickness. Someone knocked on the door; was it the doctor with a sedative? It was not; it was Angus, a Scottish friend I had not seen for years; he had come to wish me good luck. 'You'll need it', he said with a knowing smile; to date he has been married three times. When he lived as one of my near neighbours he made his second wife pregnant for the first time when calling on her to discuss the divorce arrangements; oh dear – it was a bad omen.

There was another knock on the door. It was my best man, Roger Phillippo, one of the finest glass engravers in the country. Normally he is a complete extrovert; now he looked

13

ill – like me he was already on an aspirin/whisky cocktail and he wanted more.

During the course of a normal year I speak to thousands of people on rural issues up and down the country. At the Countryside Rally in 1997 I addressed 125,000 people, without one nervous twitch; now I was two-thirds of the way to becoming a gibbering idiot.

As I prepared to take off into another life, time seemed to accelerate. 'Let's get going', Roger said, wanting another whisky, but fearing the breathalyser. I boarded his ancient, ribbon-strewn Citroën. Of course it wouldn't start – I felt sick. After a quarter of an hour of cursing and cajoling, the motor burst into life, but we were now late and only just beat the bride out of her gate. At the church the Rev Peter Owen-Jones looked relieved – he had thought he was about to conduct a wedding with no bride and no groom. He smiled – his hair looked as wild and wildlife friendly as Roger's and mine. As usual he was wearing his favourite jeans and winkle-picker shoes under his cassock. He is currently filming the second series for BBC 2 entitled 'The Battle for Britain's Soul'. 'I shan't watch it', Roger informed him, trying to break the tension. 'I'm not interested in fishing.'

The bride arrived on a sleigh drawn by the best Cairngorm reindeer, accompanied by Alan and Tilly Smith, Britain's only reindeer herders. The reindeer looked beautiful – but so did Anita. Soon I was at the altar; there was a commotion and the bridesmaid kissed me. She composed herself and we got on with the service. In no time at all I was a married man and the Register was signed. Under column five 'Rank or Profession', the Rev Peter described Anita as an 'All round good egg'. Then we were standing outside the church and I was in a complete daze. At this point the bridesmaid disgraced herself again by throwing up on the grass before jumping at me with love and admiration, knocking me to the ground. She was of course my wonderful Cambridgeshire foxhound Corset, whom I had 'walked' as a puppy and with whom I have remained friends. Her collar bore a simple message for the Prime Minister: 'I'm not a Foxhound Mr Blair, I'm a Bridesmaid'. The best man behaved almost as badly as the bridesmaid, sneaking a camera shot up Alan's kilt; needless to say it was in the cause of science – and thanks to modern camera technology it is true what they say about that murky region beneath a Scotsman's kilt.

A wild party followed – friends and relations, conservationists, farmers, villagers and anti-Europeans – as diverse as hedge layer extraordinary 'Badger' Walker, 'Scouser' Bill, 'Spaghetti Head', Graham Wynne, head of the RSPB, Zac Goldsmith, MEP Nigel Farage and Rory McGrath. The wedding cake was four tiers of chocolate, covered in Maltesers and the entertainment was provided by the great Norfolk folk singer Sid Kipper, followed by the evergreen Wurzels. Young and old alike pranced about to old intellectual favourites such as 'The Champion Dungspreader', 'Combine Harvester' and 'I am a Cider Drinker'. To the relief of all, John Morgan the 78-year-old drummer survived another rollicking rustic performance and Tommy Banner managed to stop his trousers from falling down completely.

To avoid sabotage on our wedding night we decided not to go home, or to a hotel. Instead, after a very happy day we sneaked off to my camper van (the 'passion wagon') in the farmyard, behind the cowshed. As we turned out the light a tawny owl hooted. It was cold; the windscreen was covered with ice and we shivered; we could have done with that terrier.

But that is not all; every traditional wedding – well nearly traditional wedding – must have a traditional honeymoon and soon we were lying under palm trees and eating open prawn sandwiches next to the Indian Ocean at The

Driftwood Club, Malindi, on Kenya's wonderful coast. Thanks to the generous help of Mr Blair's heating allowance, I was managing to keep warm. Other dangers lurked however; in the dead of night, the flimsy bed broke without warning; I still do not understand how that happened. Then one evening I was horrified, suddenly noticing a little black face with his nose pressed to the window of our hut and his eyes out on stalks – he had evidently never seen synchronised aerobics before.

Back in Nairobi we stayed with my old friend, safari guide Joe Cheffings. When he first arrived in Kenya in the early 1950s the Kenyan population was just five million; now it is over 30 million. The expats were all greatly amused by the reported profundities emanating from our dear Prime Minister 'Bomber' Blair, and his rival, Gordon Brown, on the subject of Africa; they found it even more entertaining than the cricket on television. I wonder if either Africa visionary has read an article in Kenya's *Daily Nation* on January 17th, 2005 by Martin Shikuku, a former Kenyan MP. When Kenya received its independence in 1963 its infrastructure was in place, its economy was healthy and its administration worked. Now forty years later Martin Shikuku writes, 'Without a doubt, my worst decision was my participation in the fight for Kenya's independence. It is very difficult to acknowledge that I participated in chasing away white rule only to bring black leadership that has made our people poorer than they were. If ever I had known that our struggle against colonialism would result in making Kenya more impoverished, I would not have participated in it. There were better things I could have done than this. I believe Kenya would have been better off under the British than under indigenous rulers, and those like me who participated in kicking out the colonialists having joined politics at the age of 19, feel so wasted.'

Oh dear – I bet Tony and Gordon will never talk to him and he will certainly not be interviewed by the BBC.

Joe lives in a little community of conservationists and safari guides on the edge of Nairobi: 'Look Anita – there goes Jonathan Scott of *The Big Cat Diaries*'; 'Look Anita, there goes Esmund Bradley Martin the world's leading authority on the ivory trade'; 'Look Anita, there goes Mark Rose, a mate from Cambridge – Mark Rose? Oi, what are you doing here?' Mark is Director of Fauna and Flora International and he said: 'We've got a fantastic project under way up north – come and see it; it is just right for your honeymoon.'

We landed on a dusty, hot airstrip in the Laikipia region of Northern Kenya: 'Did we land on that?' Anita gulped. She gulped several times more; we had landed in the middle of the 69,000-acre Ol Pejeta Ranch. Yes the wildlife was fantastic – elephants, lions, buffaloes and Anita's favourite, the Go-Away bird. But far more impressive than all the animals was the honeymoon bed in the old ranch house. Oh dear, this had once been the holiday home of the arms dealer and playboy Adnan Kashoggi. The bed we were given was an enormous 12ft by 12ft; a safari guide was needed to get from one side to the other. Next door was the bathroom cum dressing room, with a bath big enough for four, and a concealed door in a wardrobe which led to the room where video cameras had once been.

Over the dinner table was a large boat shaped basket. In the good old days it had contained a naked girl who was then lowered onto the table for dessert. Anita declined the invitation to climb aboard and after a proper dessert we went to bed. What an experience – it took an age to find my bride in the vast expanse of sheets – then, once found, it was a major crawl to the edge of the bed to switch off the bedside lamp. By the time I had found her again I was so exhausted that I fell asleep. Any undiscovered cameras would have been very disappointed.

Two days later we had our first real mishap. After the exciting experience of approaching black rhino on foot the day before, I was clearly overconfident and was charged – the rhino at Lewa Downs just caught my leg. Fortunately she was only eight-month-old Tula, being hand reared and already drinking five pints of milk from a large bottle five times a day. She was born to a blind mother named Mawingu (meaning 'cloud' in Swahili). Because of her lack of sight, two of her earlier calves had been killed by a hyena and a leopard. Consequently when Tula was found alone two days after birth it was decided to adopt her. With three guards covering every hour of the day she is now safe and well fed. At night she sleeps with a blanket, next to one of her guards, and she refuses to go to sleep unless one is there.

Almost at the end of the honeymoon near disaster struck – toothache. It meant an emergency rush to Mr Desai, an Asian dentist in Nairobi. 'Would you like to come in and watch?', they asked Anita. Toothache was being turned into a spectator sport. With forceps raised he smiled: 'Are you feeling all right?', he asked Anita (not me) and the large molar was painlessly extracted – the only thing missing was a lady with a tray selling ice creams and a programme.

So as we caught the plane home, my change of life was complete. The wanted quad bike will have to wait another year but who cares? To me my marriage has been great, less painful and more entertaining than my visit to Mr Desai, and, if I am honest, neither the terrier nor Mr Blair's heating allowance are really wanted.

4

What an Otter

Otters have been an obsession of mine for years. As a boy I walked the brook banks on the southern boundary of the farm several times a week and spent hours sitting close to an old waterside tree that fishermen claimed was a holt, but I saw no sign of that elusive whiskery face. I shed buckets of tears when reading Henry Williamson's classic, *Tarka the Otter*, but the otter remained an animal of fiction and of Tunnicliffe's wonderful woodcuts. Later, when writing my first book on country sports, *The Hunter and the Hunted*, I went out with two otter hunts, but by then mink and coypu had become the quarry – clever scientists and ignorant politicians had managed to wipe out virtually all the otters in England and Wales through the irresponsible use of pesticides. 'Silent spring' meant silence for birds and animals alike.

I walked miles in North Norfolk searching for the last of East Anglia's otters with the Hon. Vincent Weir, whose charity the Vincent Wildlife Trust did much valuable monitoring work. Then I saw real otters, as Philip Wayre began his captive breeding programme near Bungay, through his Otter Trust. Over time I experienced the thrill of seeing genuine wild otters on Rhum, Islay and Shetland. I even saw a distant English otter after a long wait at the RSPB's Leighton Moss reserve in Lancashire.

In Suffolk, after DDT and Dieldrin had been banned, I saw a release pen on the farm of John Wilson, where the first of Philip Wayre's captive bred otters were to be released in 1983. I went too with Jeremy Sorensen, the then warden of the RSPB's Minsmere reserve to see spraints (droppings) and footprints after a successful release there.

I thought nothing more about otters locally – believing that we were lumbered with mink, until a memorable knock on my front door in 1993. A pretty blonde girl announced that we had otters. Being a born-again know-all I told her that she was mad and that we had mink – but she took me down to the brook bridge and showed me an otter spraint – a beautiful, sweet smelling otter spraint. Indeed the Suffolk re-introduction had been a success and otters had spread along the river and drainage systems of Suffolk, Cambridgeshire and the Fens and into the Cam and its tributaries. That first sniff of spraint was memorable – like bloater paste – that good. It is ironic that as otters have come back from the very edge of extinction – so bloater paste seems to have become extinct.

That sniff of spraint led to the launch of the Countryside Restoration Trust and we soon bought our first 20 acres with 400 yards of brook bank to be made otter friendly. We launched in *The Daily Telegraph* on July 24th 1993 and the field is still called Telegraph Field through the generosity of Telegraph readers. Now that chunk of land has spread to nearly 400 acres with two and a half miles of otter friendly brook bank. But although there are many signs of otters, the otters themselves have remained elusive.

Then suddenly one night recently the telephone rang at 10.15pm. It was a friend who lives in a neighbouring village – two miles as the crow flies and three miles as the otter swims. 'Come over now', Brian said in a whisper, 'they're here.' Lulu, my new wife, looked at me in amazement as I bundled her into the car. Her amazement increased; thirty yards from the Rhee (a tributary of the Cam), Brian has a lake containing decreasing numbers of koi carp and golden orf, and there in the spotlight, were my first definite sightings of wild Cambridgeshire otters – three of them – using the lake as a branch of Harry Ramsden's. Despite the light they swam, dived and chattered to one another totally unconcerned, sometimes as close as just ten yards away. It was astonishing. They were beautiful and the experience was well worth the wait of the best part of a lifetime; it was also far and away the best wedding present we had.

Since then Brian has had four otters simultaneously fishing his lake. Tony Norman, a farming CRT friend in Herefordshire reports similar unconcerned otter behaviour, several times a year, in the stream that runs through his farm. It leads to visitors saying: 'And it is so nice of you having those tame otters in your stream Mr Norman.'

5

Goodbye – Friend and Inspiration

I heard of Miriam Rothschild's death in Kenya; I was upset. I had intended to see her before I left, but had put it off. 'I'll see her on my return' – it is a delay that I will always regret. I first met her in 1981. I stopped outside the Chequered Skipper pub in Ashton Wold, that model thatched village in Northamptonshire built by her father, to ask the way: 'Oh, the Honourable Miriam Rothschild', the villager observed with a smile, 'she may be an Honourable but she looks more like a gypsy peg-seller. She lives down the road; as it's the only house along there, the road becomes their private drive.'

The large stone built house, covered with roses and climbing plants was set among tall trees and overgrown lawns. I was ushered into the library by a man wearing Wellington boots; Miriam was instantly recognisable, reclining on an old sofa and wearing a headscarf, smock and tasteful yellow galoshes, but without the basket of pegs. She immediately started to talk about butterflies – how drifting sprays were killing them off and how she had changed the name of the 'Three Horseshoes' pub to the 'Chequered Skipper', as that had once been a beautiful, endangered butterfly to be found at Ashton Wold. I had expected to hear about fleas by this self-taught expert, but unlike orthodox, formally trained 'experts' Miriam hadn't got tunnel vision, she had moved on. What was happening to butterflies could happen to us – they were an 'indicator species'. We had to get the message across – we had to broaden the whole concept of conservation to cover all land – farm land, moorland, not just nature reserves. This was coming from the woman whose father founded The Society for the Promotion of Nature Reserves.

Each subsequent visit to Ashton Wold became both a privilege and an adventure – what was the latest project? Restoring hay meadows; flowering school grounds and roadside verges; planting the wild pear in our hedgerows; dragonflies; encouraging wild roses; converting farmers; convincing politicians; 'come and see this' and 'I hope you are coming to my summer party'. Each June she had a party for locals, friends, farmers and conservationists to encourage them to co-operate, exchange ideas and enjoy themselves. For several years I gave up a cricket match to attend, fearing it may be the last – then last year I did miss it – and it was the last. Miriam herself loved cricket and once played for England's women's team – appearing under an assumed name to avoid the wrath of her father. Her love of sport extended further; being an insomniac she only had two or three hours' sleep a night: 'How do you spend your nights?' I once asked her. 'I love watching sport on Sky', came the unexpected reply.

She did not suffer fools lightly. On one occasion I was filming a piece with her for Anglia Television. Fed up with the Basil Fawlty qualities of the producer she announced at 11.30: 'I have friends coming for lunch at 12.30 and will not be coming out this afternoon.' Suddenly the producer's mind cleared, but exactly at 12.30 she said: 'Thank you very much. That's filming over – goodbye. Robin, would you like to join me for lunch?' As I passed, the producer muttered: 'Don't worry – while you are all inside we'll get extra footage by filming in the garden without her knowing.'

Once lunch had started Miriam said: 'I suppose they're filming in the garden now and they think I don't know.'

Politicians did not impress her. She regarded Tony Blair as being remarkably shallow. On being told of the problem of declining farmland birds he said: 'I'm interested in people, not birds'; she was unimpressed. She was a vegetarian, not because she was against meat eating, but she objected to the way in which farm animals are treated and slaughtered. She was appalled by BSE and the Government's hysteria over foot-and-mouth, and John Gummer's ears must have regularly burnt over his closure of slaughterhouses through absurd EU rules. She was a great supporter of mobile slaughterhouses and was disappointed that the idea was never given the government support it deserved.

When the CRT was launched in 1993 she was particularly encouraging and our first restored hay meadow was, and is, a flowering tribute to her vision. She was always a listener on the end of a phone offering ideas, advice and solutions. When I last saw her she was frail but still enthusiastic with ideas to get conservation into schools; she was 96: 'Although my father would have said that I was 97 – he measured age from the time of conception.'

In an age when mediocrity seems to be the order of the day she was a remarkable woman and as unfashionable as it may be, to me she was a hero – or even a heroine. Although, when the news of her death came through I was on my honeymoon, I shed a tear for Miriam Rothschild in Africa.

6

Manic Organic

It is with trembling fingers that I type this chapter; I want to be loved, but I am sure that I will offend some delicate readers. The reason is simple: I am not organic – that applies to me personally and to my farm. If I am ill and go the doctor, when he gives me medicine I do not say 'Is this organic? – I will only have organic medicines', because I want to recover as quickly as possible and I know that the treatment given to me will be some sort of synthesised chemical. In fact I have never heard anybody at the local medical centre show any concern about how their medicine has been produced – they want to take it as soon as possible, and recover. Yet a growing number of people expect me as a farmer to only use organic solutions with my livestock and crops. In other words they apply one set of standards for themselves and expect me to use an entirely different set of standards when treating my sheep or trying to get rid of ragwort in my grass. I do not understand it.

Furthermore, every day I take inhalers to help control my

asthma. I have never asked where the chemicals come from or what they were tested on – I am happy to be alive and active. It is not funny having had more bouts of bronchitis and pneumonia than I can remember and I am just glad that medical and chemical science have kept me going this long. I hope too that they keep me alive for another twenty years; I want to continue being a thorn in the flesh of our political, farming and conservation establishments – they deserve it.

In my farming I do not throw chemicals about rashly, I use them sensibly, when I need them – as does the Country-side Restoration Trust on its Lark Rise Farm. I am glad the vet came and used something potent on a desperately ill lamb last autumn – because as a result it is still with us today. I use no chemicals on my old water meadows – except 'spot-spraying' nettles, thistles and ragwort, because I do not want chemical residues or spray getting into the river system. This is not being 'organic', it is being responsible and using common sense. If I have a field that becomes infested with couch grass – which we in Cambridgeshire call 'twitch' – then I have no hesitation in using 'Roundup', despite it being manufactured by what I regard as the evil empire of 'Monsanto'; I believe that it is the most wildlife friendly way of getting rid of this troublesome weed.

When my late father was farming the farm, twitch was a nightmare. He would leave a field fallow and harrow it for the whole of the summer – using gallons of diesel, numerous man hours and putting the nests of skylarks and English partridges at serious risk, as well as almost certainly killing many leverets. Three years later the twitch would be back. Today we pass over the field just once – the problem is solved and little damage is caused. That is why I believe that if a bird and butterfly survey were to be done on Lark Rise Farm – with the Trust's grass margins, unsprayed headlands and beetle banks – but sprayed crops – we would have more wildlife than that found on a purely organic farm. Many organic farmers have to disc harrow their clover into the ground in midsummer – at key lark nesting time; and organic cereal growers also mechanically hoe their crops at the height of the breeding season to get rid of weeds such as charlock – destroying lark nests and young as they go. The CRT is developing an organic smallholding in Norfolk (we are not against organics – we are interested in trying to improve all types of farming) but we did have to stop discing last June because of the number of nesting larks.

My biggest grouse against organic farming concerns the killing of livestock. I have always believed that my sheep and cattle should be killed as close to the farm as possible to avoid fear and stress. Ideally I would like a mobile slaughterhouse to visit the farm – but enthusiasm for these seems to have disappeared through cost and EU regulation. When the butcher I supplied became 'organic', he had to start using an 'organic slaughterhouse' – a slaughterhouse that pays an annual levy to the Soil Association. Because of this, the miles my near organic animals had to travel to be slaughtered increased from 25 miles to 75 miles. Consequently on principle, even if I had wanted to be registered 'organic', I would not have done so, as I will not send my animals to the distant abattoir.

So, I am not organic, and I feel very well this winter with the help of my chemical puffers. My little farm is not organic either – and it is teeming with wildlife and my sheep and cattle have happy healthy lives. As a result, as the barn owls and tawny owls hunt, I sleep very well, with a clear conscience.

7

Hare Today

Spring is sprung, the sap is rising, the rooks are calling, the violets are flowering and the mad March hares are certainly living up to their reputations; and there is no doubt that brown hares really do go mad in March. It is the month when love seems to dominate their lives and the more erotic both male and female become, the more erratic their behaviour. They run in circles at high speed; they jump and turn in mid-air and they appear to box. Sometimes there can be just two of them; at other times there can be a dozen (sorry to use this politically incorrect, non-Europeanised form of counting) or even more.

The other day I was watching this madness under a full moon. It was incredible. Fifteen hares running, boxing and generally behaving badly – yes, hares behaving badly, as if they had been released too early from an animal mental institution. Because the hare has large bulging eyes towards the side of its head, it is thought that a sitting hare has almost 360-degree all-round vision, while a running hare can actually look backwards. During one part of the madness two hares appeared to be running flat out at top speed (which can be nearly 50 mph); it seemed as if they must collide head on but at the last minute they both jumped high in the air, twisted and missed. What all that was about, I have no idea; whether they had both been bucks (males) sprinting to impress a female (a doe), and had been looking backwards until the last minute; or whether it was a hare game of 'chicken' I haven't the foggiest idea. That is part of the attraction of the brown hare; although it is one of our commonest animals it remains one of our most mysterious.

Gradually however some of the mysteries are being solved. For instance at one time it was thought that not only did hares go mad during March, but they also became mentally challenged during a full moon. This can be explained by the fact that many of the tales concerning hares were started generations ago when Britain was predominantly rural. Before the age of electricity the only time hares would be seen at night would be under a full moon – the chances are that their behaviour was just as bizarre at other times too, but they could not be seen; it is as simple as that.

There is no doubt that the brown hare is one of our most well loved and attractive animals, but sadly it is also one of our most threatened. Small changes in farming practice; in-considerate use of chemicals and disturbance by too many people walking pet dogs off leads during the main leveret time (the young of hares are called leverets) can all cause immense problems. Indeed during the 1970s and 1980s extinction seemed to be a certainty. On my small Cambridgeshire farm, hares disappeared completely and my little lurcher dog, Bramble, the traditional gypsy dog, renowned for chasing hares, didn't see one until he was twelve. Then when a hare got up and ran in front of him he just stood and watched in amazement. I could almost read his mind: 'Good heavens what was that? That was a big, fast rabbit.'

The almost total disappearance of the hare was caused by the intensification of farming, at the behest of ignorant politicians who claimed to love wildlife and then encouraged farming methods that wiped it out. Acres of intensively farmed cereals flattened leverets, and the sprays poisoned the adults. Then with mass autumn cultivation, when all the land was ploughed and there was no food, hare numbers plummeted. Fortunately the introduction of set-aside gave hares some respite – giving them areas for feeding and breeding without disturbance. Farming and conservation charities such as the Countryside Restoration Trust (CRT) have also initiated farming methods with grass margins, meadows and spring-sown crops that have allowed hare numbers to climb back to their peak. It is ironic that at the same time as this environmentally illiterate Government is paying scientists thousands of pounds to bring the brown hare back under its grandly titled Biodiversity Action Plan, the CRT has achieved it for nothing. Similarly the intensification of grass farming, in which grass is repeatedly cut throughout the summer for silage, has led to the hare population being decimated. The CRT now has farms in Herefordshire and hopes to bring hares back to grassland too.

When I was a boy, hares were ten a penny, and I remember finding a small leveret so young that it could settle into the palm of my small hand – it had just been born. Baby rabbits are born safely under ground, hairless and pink; hares that live above ground are born already covered with fur, with their eyes open. There can be as few as one in a litter, or as many as eight. One old country tale says that if a leveret has no white spot on its forehead it is single – if it has a white spot, it is one of several. Another tale suggested that because the young leveret is so vulnerable to predators – dogs, foxes, buzzards, crows and so on – the doe drops her young separately and feeds them singly. Norfolk farmer and Survival film-maker, Chris Knights, disproved this; he witnessed a doe giving birth to her four young in the same place. However, as soon as their fur was dry, the young leverets crept off in different directions. Some people believe that the female feeds her young separately, but naturalist Bob Burton has witnessed a female call up her young at feeding time – no fewer than eight turned up to their mobile milk bar.

When I attended my village school over fifty years ago, there was still much folklore alive and well concerning the hare. For years one of the boys in my class carried a hare's foot in his pocket for luck. This is said to date back to the time of Noah's ark. Apparently the ark sprang a leak – so Noah, at his wits' end, cut the foot off a hare and bunged the hole up with it. What a good job none of his sons were members of the RSPCA. It is also a fact that it is very difficult to tell the difference between a male and female hare, even when cut up for the pot – delicious 'jugged hare'. As a result many country people believed that hares changed sex month by month at full moon. This too dates back to Noah. On leaving the ark, one of the pair of hares saved from the Flood fell into a puddle and drowned, causing the remaining hare to become both sexes at the same time. It is possibly because of this sexual confusion that traditional country people always refer to a hare as 'she', often calling 'her' 'Sally', 'Sarah', or more infrequently 'Puss'. In much the same way a fox is usually called 'Charlie'.

Because of the hare's wild eyes and wild behaviour it was thought by people in remote areas that hares could turn themselves into witches. In the Fens old shepherds feared hares because of their links with witches and it is said that there is not one 'Hare and Hounds' pub in the Fens because of this superstition. A hare running through a house was supposed to warn of death while a hare running down a village street was supposed to precede a fire – which in the days of thatched roofs was common anyway.

Although leverets are very beautiful and cuddly they are notoriously difficult to rear as pets. One of my neighbours tried it. The experiment was successful until the beautiful animal chewed through the television's electric cable.

So this Easter go and enjoy a country walk and try to enjoy seeing a mad March hare. If as you walk you see a clod of dirt, which gets bigger as you approach it – that is a clod of dirt. If you approach a clod of dirt that seems to get smaller as you approach it – that is a hare, crouching lower. Suddenly it will spring to life – running gracefully and fast. What a relief that this beautiful and fascinating animal is now coming back as a welcome part of our countryside.

8

Swimming Against the Flow

———

It's tough work planning a revolution even with email, fax and mobile phone. People drop out at the last moment; they don't read their emails and they misread the calendar. I'm sure that in an earlier age most of my would-be revolutionary friends would have arrived at the Gunpowder Plot just in time to see the smoke rising from Guy Fawkes's very own bonfire, and if they had been very quiet they would have heard the last gasp of poor old double-crossed Wat Tyler.

Never mind, the other day a few of us wanting revolution because of the thousands of new houses promised, airport expansions, the demise of farming and the hunting ban, decided to tilt at a new urban windmill. We decided to protest against the London Olympics; if urban Britain interferes with our rural lives, why shouldn't we interfere with a few metropolitan lives, particularly as all the political and media establishment in London are supporting these crazy, expensive games. I wonder if Ken Livingstone will want synchronised newt racing as part of his special contribution? In addition, of course, the London Olympics will suck money away from the rest of the country and where will the lottery money be for my village's new pavilion and for the resurfacing work on the tennis courts?

I believe that in any case the Olympics should be held in the developing world, with the rich countries paying for new facilities and improved infrastructure in the country chosen. This would be one positive way of helping to overcome poverty and improve lives. It is a simple message – but a bit too simple for all those intending to make money out of the Olympics. Instead of 'Make Poverty History', as far as the London Olympics are concerned it is 'Make Money Now'.

So what should we do? Should The Countryside Against the London Olympics plan muckspreaders at dawn in Parliament Square, and would Farmers For Action want to take part? Sadly they never rang back, preferring to be Farmers for Inaction on the chosen day. We decided that the best way to show our discontent at this early stage was a letter to the Prime Minister, personally delivered, outlining his many sins, which make London a most inappropriate place for the Olympics.

Strangely, permission to deliver letters to 10 Downing Street comes from the Government's 'Events Office' – we were to become an 'event'. Six volunteers (the permitted number) were lined up, including reindeer herder Tilly Smith, a former Under-23 hockey international and Zac Goldsmith, who would be in any British Olympic team if only poker was an Olympic sport. I would like to throw mangold-wurzels for Britain, but I haven't seen a 'mangold' for years. With a day to go both had dropped out; Tilly had forgotten to get a ticket from Scotland and Zac had forgotten a meeting. Chaos – eventually Tilly managed to get a ticket to lovely Luton; and lovely Lulu my new wife was persuaded to become a revolutionary for the very first time in her life.

The morning of the big day dawned; 'Don't forget your teeth', Lulu said, as wives do in this 'toothist' world. Sadly, after yielding yet another gnasher to the dentist, it meant 'Polirip'. 'Don't get it on your lips', Nigel said, 'you won't be able to open your mouth all day.' Farmer Tim looked traumatised; it was only his third train ride to London in over twenty years – he would rather have been on his tractor drilling beans; instead he had chosen to be on the front line of the revolution.

Outside Number 10, things were as expected media-wise; we were virtually ignored. Instead there were around twenty young people from Kent who had read about the delivery on the Internet: 'Yes', they said, 'London gets everything – for what they're doing to the countryside they shouldn't get the Olympics.'

We delivered our letter, ate pasties on the train back and out of sixty press releases just three small pieces appeared in the press. Who cares? I'm glad we did it. It gave Tony Blair something to read and as Tilly said as she went back to Luton airport 'Somebody had to do it and I am glad to have been part of it; when's the demonstration?'

9

The Humble Bumble

Suddenly our fields and gardens are full of the sound of humming – not happy shepherds and gardeners, but bumble-bees, buzzing as they bumble along the hedgerows looking for an early taste of nectar. They need a feed, as all the early buzzers are females, 'queens' who have spent the winter hibernating somewhere safe. Then as soon as the temperature starts to rise, they are among the first of Britain's wildlife to wake and announce the approach of spring. Each year I eagerly anticipate the glimpse of my first 'bumble'; this year I spotted it on March 13th – the day after the first frogs spawned in the farm pond. Since then the few warm days over Easter have brought out these beautiful queen bumblebees in huge numbers. On a balmy Easter Day there were over twenty feeding on the sweet smelling blossom of 'pussy willow' by our little brook; I heard them before I saw them – the whole tree seemed to be humming – in sunlight, a musical tree!

These early queens are the females of the buff-tailed bumblebee – Britain's largest bumblebee. Its Latin name is *Bombus terrestris* which means 'of the earth', possibly because its colonies are usually underground – often in the old holes of mice and voles. But how can a bumblebee be beautiful? The answer is simple: just look at a bumblebee – it is fantastic. Their colours and stripes are amazing; they are covered with hair and their shape and weight should defy flight yet they fly fast, even in high winds and their manoeuvrability is astonishing. At times they seem to climb vertically at speed; at other times, when they have overshot a sweet smelling flower they almost hover; and in a wind, when the flower heads are moving they can land in the flowers with astonishing accuracy. The tall foxglove is a favourite bumble-bee flower and they seem to fit the flower tubes perfectly – but even when they are swaying in a stiff breeze, the flying skill of the bumblebee enables it to never miss the entrance.

Another flower that is a favourite of the bumblebee is the wild carrot. When the sun is out the white flower head is flat and warm; at dusk and in cool weather the flower will curl up, looking almost like a small nest. It is said that if a bumblebee is out too late to return to its colony, it will creep into the curled flower of the wild carrot for shelter during the night.

There are twenty-two types of bumblebee in Britain and now a new book has been published to help identification and to raise the profile of the bumblebee. The humble bumble needs its profile raising too. It has been estimated that up to eighty per cent of our food depends on the pollinating skills of the bumblebee, from apple and plum blossom that gives us fruit directly, to red and white clover which produces hay and grazing for sheep and cattle (lamb and beef).

Bumblebees are to be found all over Britain. Last year I puffed and struggled to the top of Ben Nevis; and what flew over when I was collecting my breath at the top? A bumblebee. I have seen them on remote islands; along hedgerows in deepest countryside and at flower filled window boxes in the middle of towns.

I can remember as a small boy crying my eyes out through fear when a bumblebee was buzzing at my bedroom window. The poor bee was only trying to get out – away from the noise: in fact they are very peaceful creatures, using their stings defensively and not as a form of attack. I do not know anyone who has been stung by a bumblebee – unlike the victims of kamikaze honeybees and grumpy wasps.

The life cycle of the bumblebee is fascinating. Only the female survives the winter and she has already been fertilised. Once she has fed and made a nest she will lay her eggs. Through a mixture of food and muscle structure they have an unusual ability to generate heat – that is why they are among the first insects to fly in the spring, and the last to fly in autumn. This body heat also helps to brood their eggs which, when they hatch, feed on the pollen and nectar collected by the queen. The first brood develops as workers, infertile queens. Because spring food is not abundant they are under-nourished and their ovaries are stunted, making it impossible for them to breed. Once these workers are flying and foraging for food, the queen sinks into appalling political incorrectness – spending her time cleaning and tidying the nest and looking after her next brood. As the amount of nectar and pollen increases during the summer so the quality of the young improves, finally producing 'drones', the males, and finally fertile females – the new generation of queens. Of course, once the collecting workers have found sufficient nectar and pollen, they will take the shortest distance back to the colony – they will make a 'bee-line' back to the nest.

Dangers are many – badgers love eating bumblebee nests – bees, grubs, and honey – the lot. Tidy gardeners and farmers are also a menace as the nests of some species need a good cover of vegetation for protection and a too enthusiastic use of weedkiller, or the mower, is a danger to the bumblebee whether on the farm or in the suburban garden.

Some bumblebees too are a problem to their own kind, as the 'cuckoo bumblebee' (of which there are six species) shows some traits of behaviour similar to the bird after which it was named. With the cuckoo queen being unable to feed and care for its young, not having pollen-collecting sacs on its legs like most bumblebees, it will raid its neighbour's nest – kill the queen and then lay its eggs in the nest, to be brooded and looked after by the host workers. At first the workers will attack the alien queen as an intruder, but eventually they accept her as their queen.

A healthy colony of bumblebees will number between 20 and 200 individuals, whereas a working hive of honeybees will number 50,000. However, with the disappearance of millions of both wild and domestic honeybees through the destructive varoa mite, many farmers and gardeners now depend almost entirely on the friendlier bumblebee to polli-nate their crops and so bumblebee conservation is becoming increasingly important.

In the autumn some of the young males, 'the drones', will mate with a new generation of queens. After mating they die, and it is the turn of the new queens to find somewhere sheltered and secure to survive the approaching winter. The Queens have to hibernate as fat as possible to get them through the worst of the cold weather. On a warm autumn day they can often be seen on the late flowers of ivy, rich in both nectar and pollen and then they will sleep. Months later, on a warm spring day they will emerge – the cycle starts once more and my pussy willow tree will again hum in the sun.

10

Rejection or Election?

I am writing this chapter in the dark. I am writing about Parliament and elections before the assumed election this year. The fact that I am putting pen to paper now is in no way sinister, but it so happens that this spring and summer I want to start the research for a new book. This will involve travelling to the four corners of Britain, not sitting in my study gazing out of the window waiting for the election. It is of course extremely irresponsible to belt about Britain emitting various greenhouse gases but I justify it on the grounds that in the event of the sea level rising, virtually the first place to be flooded out will be the House of Commons.

At one time, when I was young, I looked upon the House of Commons and the people who were elected to it in awe. It represented freedom and democracy; it really was 'the mother of all Parliaments' – I was proud to be British. Now when I walk past I feel nothing but contempt; Westminster is not the mother of Parliaments – Iceland was ahead of us – and I have come to realise that the people elected into Parliament are not representing 'us', most of them are representing small party political interests and themselves – and doing very well out of it financially at the same time thank you very much.

Before being accused of imagined party political bias I had better give my political lack of pedigree. On my father's side there were Methodists, high churchmen and atheists; there were also Tories, Liberals and cynics – almost a complete mixture. On my mother's side there was more stability – dominated by Methodism and voting Conservative. During my childhood and adolescence I was fascinated by politics from a very early age and by my teens I was a practised heckler at political meetings. Then, would-be politicians still held meetings in the village hall and I went with my friends, not to be impressed, but to be entertained by the inter-ruptions. It meant that the questions and interventions had to be well thought out to prevent the instant political put-down and humiliation. From these mini-meetings we travelled on into Cambridge – to the Guildhall – to heckle at George Brown and Vic Feather (remember them?) and Ted Heath. It was almost as good as watching Cambridge United.

By 1979 politics had severely damaged my health, and my judgement, and I stood as a Tory candidate in the 1979 General Election in Bethnal Green. Friends had said: 'Do well in a lost cause and by the next election you will get a safe seat.' I did very well in the lost cause, saving my deposit and getting the second highest swing to the Conservatives in the country. Instead of inspiring me to search out a safe seat for the next election the experience had precisely the opposite effect. Yes, during the election campaign I met many pleasant ordinary people – but I also met many thoroughly unpleasant would-be politicians from all three main parties who would have sold their grannies if it had resulted in one more vote.

Consequently next time round I was busy writing a book – *The Wildlife of the Royal Estates* – which I regarded as being far more important than the election – and in any case I was already having serious doubts about not only the Tories, but also about our political system.

I have come a long way since then; yes I am standing at the election on an un-winnable anti-EU ticket – but my involvement is based on conviction rather than ambition and my disillusionment with the three main parties and our so-called system of democracy is complete. As far as I can see, none of the main parties are interested in the countryside, farming or traditional country people; there are not enough votes in it. The Tories claim to be the party of the countryside, but they were the government that started the demise of farming through implementing various absurdities from Brussels. What the Tories started, Labour has finished, while the Lib-Dems remain a party of suburbia – interested in population densities and voting potential rather than people and minority issues; and make no mistake – countryside issues are now minority issues. Eighty per cent of Britain is countryside, yet 90% of the population is urban.

And so what must we do to get fairer representation and restore 'democracy'? Simple: instead of candidates being parachuted into safe seats where they have no local connections or interests, nobody should be allowed to stand at an election without a residential qualification; each candidate should have been living and working in their constituency for a minimum of five years. This would mean local issues and local people would be represented by one of their own kind instead of an incoming Oxbridge career politician. Simple isn't it? So simple that none of those MPs who want to reform the House of Lords, the monarchy and so on will want to reform their own undemocratic gravy train.

11

A Mole in a Hole

Moles – I like moles. I am not a born-again bunny-hugger, nor a mole hugger – but I do not understand why so many people hate moles. Moles remain largely unseen; they get on with their lives underground doing no harm to anybody or anything, apart from worms who form their main course, and garden and farm pests such as wireworms and slugs, which they have as dessert. Yet most people hate them – or at least hate the molehills they create, which give away their presence. I can see a case for controlling magpies, crows and foxes. I can even see a case for ceasing to protect sparrow-hawks and badgers – but why this hatred of beautiful, soft, minding-their-own-business moles?

I had better explain. Magpies, crows and foxes all do damage to birds and animals that often need our help and protection; magpies and crows, for instance, love the eggs of garden birds such as song thrushes and blackbirds. Foxes will eat anything that is available from ground nesting avocets and skylarks to young hares (leverets) and even domestic kittens. Sparrowhawks – a protected species – can be a scourge of other protected species such as swallows and even cuckoos, and there are now so many badgers – due to a badger population explosion – that hedgehogs are becoming a rarity in some areas. The truth is that badgers love eating hedgehogs for starter, main course and pudding. So lovable Mr Brock the badger has become as big a menace to Mrs Tiggy-Winkle as the car and the container lorry.

By comparison the mole is almost harmless; its crime is the construction of molehills. As Mr Mole tunnels around for worms he has to move the loose earth in order to progress; he simply creates a small shaft and forces the disturbed soil to the surface forming the molehill. Due to the fact that the soil has been moved and broken up, this disturbed earth can be easily flattened or scraped up and put into flowerpots, as molehill soil is excellent for bedding plants. Occasionally a larger molehill will be built – a 'fortress' where the young can be born. But what harm is there in all this? In reality there is some good, as mole tunnels can help aerate and drain the soil. In fact that is the only real crime of the mole. In the Fens it can burrow into protective banks, causing leaks and a risk of flooding; as a consequence there have always been mole-trappers in the Fens.

Elsewhere, however, it is the molehills that are said to cause the trouble – golfers apparently hate them on the fair-way and the putting green; this is quite extraordinary: they create numerous hazards to make their game more difficult – 'bunkers', spinneys and 'rough' – then as soon as another minor hazard appears – a molehill – they shout 'foul' and not only do they want to flatten the hills, but they want to kill the moles as well.

Similarly owners of racehorses hate moles – apparently the jumps at the Grand National are acceptable, but a molehill is an unacceptable hazard. 'Kill the moles' – that really is making a mountain out of a molehill. Despite this I only know of one case of a molehill causing real damage, when the Protestant King William fell off his horse in 1702 after the beast stumbled on a molehill. William died of his injuries, much to the delight of all Catholics, and ever since, supporters of the Jacobites and Bonnie Prince Charlie have drunk a toast to the 'little gentleman in black velvet' – for the mole's coat is just like black velvet.

Some farmers don't like moles as they say that the soil from molehills can get into their silage and spoil it, as well as damage their grass cutters; silage is made from grass cut very low down for winter cattle feed. If farmers were paid better for their milk and meat so that cattle grazed outside or were fed hay this problem would be overcome.

Finally of course some suburban minded gardeners hate moles and when they appear in the lawn or flowerbed they too immediately shout, 'Kill the moles'. It is interesting to note that the 'mole problem' is essentially a rural one – whenever town moles turned up in gardens, parks or playing fields they were exterminated years ago. In the past the simple way to control moles was with traps; mole-trappers became extremely skilful. Now however the cheapest and simplest way to control moles is with a deadly poison – strychnine – a poison that affects the central nervous system. Strychnine is an extremely dangerous substance – lethal to both wildlife and people; and here lies the problem – the EU is set to ban the poison and so the mole haters are in turmoil.

Lord Kimball set the tone in the House of Lords. In his time his Lordship has spoken much good sense, but on this occasion he seemed to be suffering from a new ailment – Mad Mole Disease. He seemed to envisage a great plague of moles. 'Without strychnine' he wailed, 'there will be a great explosion of moles throughout England.' I have news for Lord Kimball; there will never be a great plague of moles. Moles prefer pastureland and meadows – and with the decline of livestock farming in Britain, suitable mole habitat will decline. Moles are not rapid breeders either; they only have one litter a year, usually in May, when up to four young are born weighing just one-sixth of an ounce each. By the fifth week they are independent, but unlike the rat, the rabbit and the hare the young do not breed until the next year and they usually only live for three years anyway. They then have to be beware of several predators – buzzards, short-eared owls and tawny owls eat moles. Foxes and cats will also kill them, but often do not eat them, presumably because of an unpleasant taste. Moles also have a difficult time in very dry weather when they find it hard to burrow after worms and often come out onto the surface in desperation, where they are very vulnerable to predator attack. They do not like waterlogged land either, although they are very good swimmers and live on several islands around Britain.

Man was also once a predator of the mole. A mole's foot tied around the neck was said to be good for throat infections, whooping cough and rheumatism, and the fur was also greatly prized. The mole is covered with beautiful soft velvet fur. Because the mole travels backwards and forwards underground, the fur lies flat whichever way it is stroked. This once made mole fur very popular for hats; but the moles got their revenge. Many of the old hat-makers used the salts of lead and mercury to cure the skins, both of which can be absorbed into the body and cause madness – hence the Mad Hatter, in *Alice's Adventures in Wonderland*.

So not only does the mole population not increase at a particularly rapid rate, but the worried farmer or gardener can find more traditional ways of frightening off moles. Bottles placed upright in a mole tunnel will send a constant whistling wind through the passage, causing the mole to move on. Moles are also said to hate garlic and so a few pieces of chopped up garlic will often encourage them to move towards sweeter air. In the unlikely event of me being worried by any of the moles on my small farm, I think I will insert a picture of Lord Kimball into one of the tunnels to see what happens. Until then I am perfectly happy to live alongside the 'little gentleman in black velvet'.

12

Butterfly Boots

———

Eighty-five pounds is a lot of money for a birthday present, but that is what mine cost Lulu and assorted members of the family this year. It was an odd present as I don't want much; fashion doesn't interest me and so I wear my clothes until they fall to bits or the moths of my old wardrobe get them; books are an obsession which I buy myself as soon as I see them and then leave them unread, and with my expanding waistline meals out are not encouraged. So this year I went for something completely different – butterflies; well, not quite butterflies, but chrysalises – thirty chrysalises of the stunningly beautiful Green Hairstreak butterfly.

The trouble is that my *Great British Butterfly Safari* of several years ago has turned butterflies into almost an obsession, and this year has been a brilliant butterfly season so far. It is not just the butterflies themselves but also their astonishing life-cycles – the part of the spring and summer that sees them emerge, and the varied and beautiful landscapes to which they add colour. That year of chasing butterflies revealed species and places quite new to me, and one of those species was the Green Hairstreak. It was so small and delicate and I was disappointed that I had not seen it years ago. Most types of caterpillar have just one food plant, but the offspring of the Green Hairstreak have several – munching away on rock-rose, bird's-foot-trefoil, gorse, dogwood, buckthorn, bramble and several more. With a number of sheltered south facing hedgerows containing plenty of buckthorn, dogwood, bird's-foot trefoil and bramble, it seemed that the farm had several warm spots where this beautiful little butterfly ought to be or should be – hence the rather unusual birthday present.

I know that at this point assorted scientists, environmental studies graduates and conservation jobsworths will be saying: 'If the habitat is right – the species will come anyway.' Sorry, I don't believe you and in any case I can't wait that long. It seems odd; introduce flowers into a hay meadow and everybody says 'wonderful'; introduce butterflies to a hedge-row and the same people hold their hands up in horror. All I know is that two of my old heroes, Gordon Beningfield and Miriam Rothschild would have said, 'Do it', and so the deed was done. The thirty chrysalises were put along the bottom of the hedgerow and then the waiting and the tension began – would they appear?

On bright sunny days, between mid-May and mid-June, Lulu and I searched high and low. On several occasions green coloured lacewings took off, causing false optimism. There were holly blues, speckled woods and orange tips galore – but nothing more. Were the chrysalises eaten by voles, stolen by ants or what? I have no idea. Perhaps the butterflies emerged and I simply didn't see them. Never mind, I think I'll have the same birthday present next year and try again.

I failed once more when a group of four CRT members visited Lark Rise Farm. I showed them a large pile of fish scales and explained with great authority how the otters had changed from their traditional diet of eels to a menu of chub and pike. I explained the eel's extraordinary life cycle (almost like the salmon's in reverse) and how eels had now completely disappeared. They were most impressed at my encyclopaedic knowledge. When I took them under a bridge to sniff otter spraints they were impressed even more; there, hunting among submerged bricks and rocks was the largest and healthiest eel I have seen for forty years. The visitors seemed to think that I was in need of immediate residential care.

Not everything has been a failure however. My oldest cow was late calving this year and so my early morning check-ups continued into June. Often as I walked through the dew the barn owls were still hunting – the oldest nest box has four chicks and so the adults have to keep busy. One morning I got back to the house at seven and took Lulu a cup of tea in bed before getting in beside her. I told her about the old boy in the village who used to get up early to check his pigs, before going home, climbing the stairs and getting back into bed with his

pig yard boots still on. She started to laugh and rolled towards me before she suddenly screamed and shot out of her side of the bed in alarm. 'You've still got your boots on', she cried. I had to laugh – well, I thought it was funny at the time. Perhaps, after hand washing the sheet in the sink I should have had a washing machine for my birthday.

13

Alan the Wild Aberdeen Angus Bull

I have just been upset by a beefburger – a walking beef burger with a ring through its nose. It was not indigestion that upset me but raw fear – welcome to the farm, Alan the Aberdeen Angus bull. In fact Alan is so large that minced in the right way he would make several thousand burgers – but the one thing that Alan does not do is mince. He paws the ground, he roars and he charges – he certainly does not mince. Until last week I thought I had forgotten how to run – oh yes I can; not only can I run – I can sprint, jump and roll under electric fences.

Alan is only a temporary name for this massive lump of angry black beef that stands as big as a transit van; one of the problems is that he is more mobile than a transit van. We have named him Alan after our Scottish reindeer herding friend Alan Smith who, with a liking for pain and suffering is also a hill runner. Alan the bull does not need a hill, he is just a runner.

Alan has arrived, in theory, to make new friends – my cows. My girls are 'single-sucklers'; for the uninitiated this means that they are beef cows that, after giving birth, have their calves running with them, and suckling from them for the next six months. My calves then move on to a friend's farm in the Fens where they graze until they are up to 30 months old. They are then sold to a traditional local butcher. The end result is beautiful slow grown beef and in my view the single-suckler method of beef production is the most humane and environmentally friendly way of producing beef. With traditional grazing and restored hay meadows as part of the system, this method also produces wildflowers, butterflies, voles, harvest mice and barn owls; I call it 'wildfarming'. Then of course – to make the end product even better, horseradish grows as a local weed.

This year the system has also produced Alan, the stroppy bull. To get a calf you need a bull. Normally I borrow a Red Poll bull from a friend, as it is a quiet, attractive East Anglian breed. Unfortunately no Red Poll was available until later in the year and so I had no other option than to hire a bull. I thought I would go for a traditional breed – so welcome Alan. As he unloaded it from the trailer the owner said:

'He's very quiet and well mannered.' Friends have since said: 'What on earth have you got an Aberdeen Angus for? They're as stroppy as hell'. I thought an Aberdeen Angus was a small breed – I think that somewhere along the line somebody else got into the field of Alan's mother; he is huge, in all visible departments.

Our relationship began to fail from the first minute. He walked straight into the Dutch barn and started to demolish some hay bales instead of following the girls up the field. I drove him out, waving a stick and scolding him; he gave me a very old-fashioned look. Half way along the cow walk he stopped – as I was about to whack him with my stick he turned on a sixpence, waved his head about and snorted. Lulu cleared the electric fence by two feet and was away – I covered 50 yards in the opposite direction in 3.5 seconds. He then sat down and refused to move as if saying: 'I'm going nowhere and what are you going to do about it?'

It took a further twenty-four hours before the girls had managed to lure him into the brook meadows with their bovine charms and each evening I checked their welfare from the safety of the car – I think it really does need a 'bull-bar'.

After a week it seemed as if he had settled down – so one evening I walked down to the cattle. They were at the far end of the field and I called them. The girls looked up, mooed, and slowly walked towards me. Alan looked up from two hundred yards away, pawed the ground, snorted, put his head down and charged. 'Oh no – not again', I thought. 'Last year was bad enough being tossed by a cow with a newborn calf – Alan will flatten me – I don't want to die.' I retreated into the bramble covered hawthorn bushes where I was rolled over last year. 'Where's my mobile phone?' I hadn't got it. 'Where's my asthma inhaler?' I hadn't got it. Alan stood sixty yards away, looking for me – bellowing. I don't think he likes me. I sneaked under the electric fence, pushed through brambles and, when he looked in my direction pretended to be a tree.

I arrived home sweating, wheezing, cut and feeling lucky. 'Has he settled down now?' asked Lulu as I took a swig of sloe gin.

Oh dear – and in three weeks' time, if he has done his job, we have to load him into a trailer for his homeward journey. Watch this space – or read the obituary column.

14

Let us Prey

———

I have thought long and hard about this chapter; should I write it, or should I leave it? I have decided to go ahead – not to be controversial, but simply to promote some thought. Unfortunately not only is it politically incorrect to encourage this kind of thought, but it is also conservationally incorrect too. And what has inspired this train of thought? A male sparrowhawk eating a cock chaffinch on my lawn. Last year my garden was so overgrown that the birds had plenty of cover to protect them against sparrowhawk predation; unfortunately there was so much cover that the jays and magpies had a field-day sneaking up on unaware fledglings instead. So this year I opened the garden up a bit to foil the magpies, and now the sparrow-hawks have started again.

The big question is: why do some conservationists look upon birds of prey as being almost sacred, and so will not agree to control their numbers? Few have any doubts about the wisdom of saving favoured birds and animals by controlling rats, feral cats, wild mink and foxes. To include the cuddly grey squirrel on this list does cause a degree of dissent. Again, some plant lovers will describe deer as 'vermin' and red, roe, fallow and muntjac will all be shot to 'protect' orchids or coppiced stumps of ash or hazel. At a push, some conservationists will agree that magpies and crows can cause a problem to vulnerable species, but at the mention of problems caused by birds of prey, conservation correctness cuts in and the impression is given that every bird of prey must have complete protection.

In addition to this, birds of prey have also been re-introduced, without any real research being done on the possible consequences to other species. I write this as a great admirer of birds of prey; the return of the barn owl has caused me much joy. The arrival of buzzards and the red kite in this area is also appreciated, but what if resident birds of prey, as well as newcomers, cause problems to existing populations of vulnerable birds or animals?

For instance, how can a conservationist mourn the decrease in the house sparrow population and ignore the bird's name 'sparrowhawk'? It should be obvious how it got its name. In exactly the same way some conservationists will explain the demise of the hen harrier by blaming the activities of sportsmen. The truth is that the hen harrier was in trouble long before game shooting became popular because it did exactly what its name suggests – it harried hens and stole their chicks. Consequently the hen harrier was in competition with ordinary hen keepers – in those days peasants, (not pheasants) and so it was in trouble. From this it would appear that mythology forms part of our attitude towards birds of prey.

Another myth was peddled by Bill Oddie on television recently – and I like Bill Oddie and have met him several times. But he is a Londoner and I do not believe he totally understands the countryside through which he sometimes moves. He said in effect that before the disaster of dieldrin and DDT there was a high songbird population and a high sparrowhawk population. Therefore after DDT, with a now high sparrowhawk population but a low songbird population, the reason cannot be predation by birds of prey. The facts are, as virtually every countryman knows, that before DDT there were very few sparrowhawks because they were not protected, and most people with hens at the bottom of their gardens took pot shots at them. The sparrowhawks did not attack the hens, but would come in repeatedly for small chicks; consequently many householders, as well as gamekeepers, fired lead aspirins at them. So, Bill Oddie, I am afraid that pre-DDT there were many songbirds, but sparrowhawk numbers were very low.

I do not believe that sparrowhawks alone have caused the decline in songbird numbers, as modern farming methods and habitat loss are two more causes. But I do believe that hawk numbers are a contributory factor. Then again another myth is peddled: 'Predator numbers are controlled by prey – so if there was not enough food sparrowhawk numbers would drop.' This totally ignores the fact that some predators, sparrowhawks among them, have favourite foods. A fox entering a henhouse containing fifty hens and one guinea fowl will invariable take the guinea fowl. In exactly the same way conservationists at Welney, the Wildfowl and Wetlands Trust's reserve in the Fens, have noticed sparrowhawks specifically favouring snipe. When the favoured prey is almost wiped out, the predator then switches to another dinner; but if the favoured dinner comes back, the predator changes yet again and numbers are kept low, by predation. There is even a scientific name for this, 'the predator pit'. Perhaps if the Royal Society for the Protection of Birds could be renamed the Royal Society for the Conservation of Birds it would be more inclined to discuss this 'pit'.

So there we are. I am not all that worried by my eaten cock chaffinch; but I am worried by the fact that as soon as the decreasing numbers of swallows and house martins in the parish bring off their young, hunting sparrowhawks appear circling above. In addition small numbers of lapwings are very vulnerable to sparrowhawk attack and I cannot see how I can get breeding lapwings back while sparrowhawk numbers are so high. What I want to know is: am I out of step, or do readers agree with me? I think both I, and the RSPB need to know.

15

It's a Cow's Life

When am I going to be made an honorary professor? In fact when are most of the livestock farmers in Britain going to be made professors and given huge research grants? The reason I ask this is that two professors have just come up with some remarkable information that every farmer has known for years. What is remarkable is the fact that they didn't simply ask me, or one of the Archers, which would have saved them a lot of time and money. Christine Nichol, professor of animal welfare at Bristol University, and John Webster, professor of animal husbandry at the same university, have come up with the startling information that cows form friendships, become excited, work out problems and bear grudges; that, according to the professors, makes them individuals. What is more,

Professor Webster has discovered that cows become excited when one of the herd comes on heat – he describes their behaviour as like 'gay nymphomaniacs'. What a discovery! that is exactly how farmers know when to call the artificial inseminator or get the real thing – the bull.

We have always had cows on the farm and so from a very young age I was always in contact with them; in fact when I was about four that contact was much too close. My father had taken me to one of our old meadows to see a mother and a brand new calf – something that still fills me with wonder. As we were watching the calf trying to stand for the first time on its wobbling, shaking legs, our old labrador Judy turned up, never one to overlook the chance of a nice fresh heap of afterbirth. Oh dear – the dietary delights of farm dogs – how long will it be before Mrs Beckett demands that they only eat accredited Government dog biscuits, with a knife and fork of course? As soon as the dog appeared, the cow ceased to be the calm, domesticated animal, proudly licking her calf – she became a wild demented animal wanting to protect her offspring from a predator. She charged at the dog, regardless of the fact that it was directly behind me. The dog fled, I was trampled for the first time in my life. I was covered from head

to foot with a mixture of cowpat and tears and it taught me a very early lesson. The line between domesticity and the wild, in farm animals, is very fine and even in animals that have been domesticated for thousands of years similarities can be seen with genuine wild animals.

My other early encounters involved letting small calves suck my fingers. Once a calf was taken from its mother so that the mother could be milked as part of a dairy herd, it had to be taught to drink from a bucket. The way to do it simply was, and still is, to let it suck your fingers and gradually lower your hand into a bucket of warm milk. Once milk was being sucked in, the fingers were slowly withdrawn – and with luck the calf would be drinking.

In those days we actually did have a cow with a crumpled horn – she was a bully and used it to good effect on the rest of the herd, ensuring that she got the best hay and the most comfortable bed in the yard. Another was a thinker – she was always the one for whom the grass really was greener over the next hedge or hollow; she would be the one to find the gate left open – the small gap in the hedge that could be made bigger – and where she went, the rest of the herd would follow. They always seemed to get out on a Sunday – but I'm sure they never studied the calendar.

Then there was another who always seemed to be the one who would discover when the electric fence was shorting. Once she discovered the wire was harmless she would simply walk straight through it.

But many of the cows would be trusting too – letting my father and the vet help them with difficult calvings; and some with limps, or too many summer flies would come back to the yard as if to ask 'Can you do something about this please?' In those days the fact that livestock could bear grudges was shown by the bull. Twice our big old Shorthorn bull had my father down, unexpectedly, but on both occasions Father was able to roll to safety. The third time it had him down it actually started to gore him and but for the bravery of Jim the World War One veteran working on the farm, he would have been killed. But Jim, remembering his old bayonet charges, charged the bull with a pitchfork shouting: 'Get back you bugger get back'. Every year after that my father suffered from a bad back, but without old Jim's intervention he would have been six feet under. Shortly after that the bull became 'bullied beef' and we started having the artificial inseminator. He was a ginger haired man we called the 'ginger-headed bull'; yes, Professor Webster, it was the excitement of the cows that told us when 'the ginger-headed bull' should come.

So fifty years ago I think I already knew what the professors have just 'discovered'. I still have a small herd of beef cows; life would be far simpler without them but I like them both as a herd and as individuals; in addition mixed farms with livestock and permanent grass are much better for wildlife. Three young cows that were born weak and were hand reared still come up to us for conversations and patting, and they will stay in their little group within the herd. Inevitably, one of them, who will not stand her ground, will be chased away from the hay by two older dominant females. In the summer the whole herd will approach me from the fields when I call them – but if a stranger is with me or they see a stranger and an unfamiliar dog they will retreat, group together snorting and stamping, behaving exactly in the same way as wild Cape buffalos in Africa. It is a sign of how ordinary people have become detached from farm life and nature that every year, people walking through cattle, usually with dogs, are injured or even killed.

From its absurd regulations it is also clear that the Government does not understand cattle, insisting that farmers have to blood-test and ear-tag their animals in a way that breaks the usual trust between the cows and their keepers.

Every two years blood has to be taken from all cattle to test for TB and brucellosis by DEFRA order; in my view DEFRA officials should organise the tests, as they defy all rules of health and safety. The cattle have to be enclosed and put individually into a 'crush'; some individual cows will accept this calmly. Others will stamp, threaten, their cowpats will become loose through anxiety in a matter of seconds; they will try to jump five barred gates – endangering themselves, my helpers and me. One recently tried to jump a tractor – landing across the bonnet with her legs splayed out and milk squirting from her teats in all direction.

Absurdly too, ear tags have to be put on calves as soon as they are born; this is ridiculous and with some breeds it can be extremely dangerous. Last year as I was ear-tagging a newborn calf with the help of a friend, Mick, it suddenly called for its mother. The mother came at the charge, hitting me in the chest and sending me flying through the air. Once landed she was on me again, whacking me with her head and she only stopped when she decided to chase Mick instead. I was lucky, suffering only a broken rib, strains and bruises – but each year farmers and farmworkers get badly injured and even killed from this nonsense – thank you Mrs Beckett. It was not the cow's fault – she was just defending her calf – it was DEFRA's ridiculous regulations that were to blame; farmers should be given two months in which to ear-tag their calves allowing the mother's protective instincts to die down.

So thank you professors – there is a space on the wall for the honorary degree – if you want any more help with your research – don't hesitate to phone.

16

Still Head Banging

———

Blickling Hall, Norfolk, is one of the jewels in the crown of the National Trust – at least that is how the author of a tourist guide would put it. I agree that it is an incredibly beautiful place – a great 17th century Jacobean House overflowing with ancient treasures. So it was to the grounds of Blickling Hall that I went the other evening with Lulu and friends to see some remarkable visiting antiques – Status Quo, the 60s pop group, still going strong. At a time when most people their age are sipping their cocoa and searching for their slippers, these old head-bangers are still banging their heads. They don't need bus passes – they seem to have their own luxurious bus, but like me I expect that our great leader and benefactor Bomber Blair will soon be sending two of the group, Francis Rossi and Rick Parfitt, their heating allowances every winter.

It was a really 'cool' evening – thousands of people in a beautiful setting, pretending that they were young again. The rebels of the 60s have become the BMW drivers of the 21st century and, with many, smoked salmon and champagne picnics have replaced smoking 'dope' and lager hangovers. Behold, the free love generation has become the generation of free prescriptions, and in some cases too, free television licences. Good gracious, suddenly I spotted two policemen walking through the crowd; what were they up to? Possibly body searches for Sanatogen and evening primrose.

'Oi, Lulu – look at that – he can hardly walk – I hope they've got a mobile intensive care unit on the site'; that was about the level of my conversation. I suppose those around us were muttering similar pleasantries: 'Cor, look at that fat old rustic with no teeth – she must be his nurse.' By this time I couldn't have cared less – Lulu had already bought me the 'Status Quo World Tour Summer 2005' T-shirt at £20 a throw. I wish that kind Mr Blair would give me a clothing allowance.

Oh dear – and then the concert started – with a group of well-seasoned women in the audience driven to playing inflatable guitars. In their twenties they may have looked erotic – in their sixties they looked erratic and it was clear that with some the air guitars would soon be replaced by the

Zimmer frame. Lulu, in 'Dancing Queen' mode danced the night away – as did several young interlopers and it was a very enjoyable night. The old rock 'n' roll geriatrics played for two hours at a physical, musical and decibel level that could only be admired. How the beams of Blickling Hall stood up to the pounding bass guitar only a building inspector could say; and how many air guitarists were in hospital the next day, only the Norfolk ambulance service would know.

As dusk fell a late bumble flew over and a group of geese skirted the park – but what about any goldfinches trying to rear their broods in some of the nearby trees? I hope they didn't go deaf. More and more landowners big and small are holding concerts and an assortment of events as part of their farm diversification to bring in extra income. Being in the middle of July the Status Quo concert was almost all right – but what about large concerts held in the countryside earlier, in the middle of the bird breeding season? Numerous parent birds must desert and fledglings die as a direct result of concerts held in the wrong place at the wrong time. As a consequence it seems right that the Wildlife and Countryside Act should be amended to prevent the reckless and often selfish destruction of wildlife by events held during the breeding season. The Glastonbury Festival is one event that must cause immense disruption to breeding farmland birds and is distinctly 'ungreen' as a result, yet it is gleefully supported by numerous 'greenies' – the BBC and, sadly, even *The Daily Telegraph*. In August or September it would be fine – in June it is out of order.

This is not to say that people and wildlife cannot be compatible in the breeding season. One of the best wildlife experiences anywhere can still be experienced in Britain, and again courtesy of the National Trust – at the Farne Islands, off the Northumberland Coast. This year a record of over 100,000 pairs of sea birds have bred successfully, without the food shortages experienced further north. Visitors have been able to see thousands of puffins, guillemots, cormorants and terns from a distance of a few feet. Lulu couldn't decide which she liked best, the puffins or Status Quo – but it is remarkable how the National Trust is trying to safeguard both these ancient forms of wild life.

17

The Great Betrayal

———

Whatever has happened to Britain? Although this country is often heralded as a great bastion of freedom and democracy, boasting a vibrant multicultural society – take a closer look. Reality tells a different tale, of a changing Britain, a Britain which, as it becomes more suburbanised and urbanised, has forgotten its rich rural culture and the traditional country people who are part of it. We hear much about ethnic cleansing throughout the world, and it is universally condemned by civilised societies, yet in Britain, over the last few years we have been witnessing the cultural cleansing of our countryside and country people.

Even as I write, farming is dying on its feet and rural communities are being sanitised and homogenised by councillors, bureaucrats and outsiders who move in. Hunting has been banned, shooting is undoubtedly the next target, and walk along the road carrying a gun and a rabbit while wearing a fur hat, and some people look at you as if you are a mass murderer. It is a sad and sorry state of affairs in which the great British traditions of individual freedom and tolerance have been traded in, by an overpaid bunch of political jobsworths, for political correctness and Westminster Brownie Points.

There is no easy answer to the demise of rural Britain. The simple fact is that those of us who still live and work in the countryside have been betrayed. Worse still, that betrayal started not under Labour, but under the Tories. Even today the 'New Tories' are telling the world that they are no longer the party of the countryside. Tory hopeful, and, as far as I am concerned, New Labour 'sound-alike', Margot James, says 'No longer should the public see the Tories as representing a narrow band of Middle England.' Needless to say, Ms James is a London-living lesbian, with a TV presenter as her partner, and I have news for her: the Tories have not represented middle England for twenty years. If she wants an 'inclusive' party – why did it exclude the countryside years ago?

It was under the Conservatives that the seeds were sown for the demise of farming, with John Gummer being one of the guilty men. Now, astonishingly, it is John Seldom Glummer who is going to be in charge of an environmental and countryside review for David Cameron. It was Seldom Glummer who put into place idiotic European regulations that have seen the closure of hundreds of local slaughterhouses. He followed this up with the BSE fiasco. The Tories then continued on their merry way by setting cereal farming on its downward course and breaking up the Milk Marketing Board, which has proved to be a disaster for dairy farming. Worse still, as I understand it, John Major had an opportunity to sign a European derogation that would have secured the future of country sports for all time, in the same way that the Spanish protected bull fighting. He failed to deliver; the party that had been the traditional party of the countryside fiddled while New Labour lined up for power, filling their pockets with large donations from various 'antis' as they did so (about £1.2million before the 1997 General Election).

The rest is history – New Labour swept in, replacing an inept Tory Government, and their battle with the countryside began, intensified by the actions of their old class warrior bigots, with historical scores to settle and prejudices to satisfy. Consequently farming has continued on its downward spiral, hunting has been banned, the 'Right to Roam' is the political flavour of the month and shooting is now well and truly in the sights of the baying parliamentary antis. Add to this the foot-and-mouth tragedy; John Prescott behaving like 'King Concrete' with his absurd planning policies; the power of the supermarkets and the Government's plans to increase our airports, regardless of normal democratic processes, and we have a real picture of gloom and doom.

I do not hunt, shoot or fish, but to me the hunting ban is simply incredible – flying in the face of virtually every principle based upon freedom and democracy; and remember most democracies believe that defending the rights of their own minorities is important. All those marches, speeches, letters, demonstrations – all for nothing. Half a million people in the streets – completely ignored. And then the sight of the Metropolitan Police attacking innocent demonstrators; having seen police behave in exactly the same way in the Third World I was both astonished and depressed.

The great countryside marches, the early anti-hunting bills and the Government's own investigation into hunting under Lord Burns coincided with the research for my book, *The Hunting Gene*. It was a remarkable education for me and for Nigel Housden, who took many of the photographs. For the first time I saw how vital hunting was in the social life of some of our most remote rural communities – in the Lake District, Wales and the West Country; how the

Devon and Somerset Staghounds bound the communities of Exmoor together.

The fell packs in the Lake District were just as important. With livestock farming under pressure they gave the shepherds and farmers their pleasure and social contact. As an asthmatic lowlander, living just twenty-five feet above sea level, I tried to keep up with the hunting action. Needless to say I usually failed, and being overtaken by astonishingly fit eighty year-olds was the ultimate humiliation. On the rare occasions that I caught up, seeing Edmund Porter, huntsman of the Eskdale and Ennerdale foxhounds, on the high tops with his hounds, in the middle of the spectacular scenery of the Lakes was so moving. It showed me how hunting and farming were joined closely together; seeing these same hill shepherds burning their fleeces in the summer as the best option for their wool also demonstrated their financial plight.

We returned to the Lake District in 2001 to see smoke again, as the great foot-and-mouth funeral pyres smouldered – almost certainly helping to spread the virus as they did so. What a time; what a scandal; what incompetence; what a

flow of heartbroken tears. When Labour came to power one of its first actions was to set up a Public Enquiry into BSE. We are still waiting for the Public Enquiry into the farce of foot-and-mouth. We saw a whole community traumatised and then this same community had its hunting taken from it – all from the Government and party that wants an 'inclusive' society. Pull the other one, Mr Blair – it's got bells on. My farming/conservation trust (the Countryside Restoration Trust) wanted vaccination from day one; the Government knew better and slaughtered 10 million animals quite need-lessly – evidently it is a government that loves foxes but not livestock. Interestingly, two Cardiff law professors believe that 7 million animals were killed quite illegally during the 'contiguous cull'; and who said 'I'm in charge'? – why, Tony Blair of course. And has Tony Blair been prosecuted for allegedly breaking the law? Of course not. We hear much these days about the rule of law – sadly the rule of law in Britain today appears to be applied selectively.

Another alleged lawbreaker appears to be The Concrete King – John Prescott. During the election he drove past a group of Countryside Alliance demonstrators shouting 'Right to Roam. Right to Roam. Right to Roam'. In vaguely similar circumstances individuals have been successfully prosecuted for 'incitement' – but was the Concrete King prosecuted? Of course not – just the girl who, with justification, threw an egg at him; what a pity it wasn't rotten. Prescott's policies too are an outrage – building houses in the south expecting people to move to jobs – instead of moving jobs up north to areas that already have empty houses. He seems to have a remarkable contempt for the countryside and each year builds on nearly 3,000 acres of green belt land.

The object of this chapter is not to make readers depressed – but to give them a reality check. In multicultural Britain we must fight to show that country people are a clear minority with a distinctive and living culture. We must therefore continue to pester the politicians of all parties until we have the same rights and protection as any other minority in Britain.

18

White Man's Burden

It is strange writing about Africa in a book concerning the British countryside, but it needs to be done. First, I had better explain; I have a long-standing love affair with Africa, and Kenya in particular. It goes back deep into childhood when 'On Safari with Armand and Michaela Denis' appeared weekly on our nine inch black and white television screen. What a programme; I'm sure its simple formula had a much more lasting affect on its viewers than the present breed of clever-dick wildlife programmes and presenters – Jonathan Scott excluded. In addition I met some real live missionaries who spoke of witchdoctors and wildlife in a way that stirred my imagination. One accompanied his tales with postage stamps – beautiful stamps depicting exotic animals, flowers and butterflies.

My father's interest in Africa grew even stronger than mine, and at a time when it was becoming distinctly un-fashionable to become a 'white settler', or even a 'wicked white settler', he decided that he wanted to become an enlightened white settler. He wanted to trade our small damp Cambridgeshire farm, struggling on top of yards of thick gault clay, for a much larger farm under the African sun, where he would run a model farm and my mother would organise a farm school and improve the lot of the Africans.

Alas, his dream came directly after the Mau Mau uprising and although the 'For Sale' notices went up all around the farm, and he even went to Kenya for three months with help from the Kenya Agricultural Settlement Board, he was finally persuaded not to take the plunge. Looking at Africa today, it was a wise decision. In my early teens, I breathed a sigh of relief; I didn't want to leave all my friends behind and I certainly had no desire to be chopped up with a panga by any remaining doped-up dissident Mau Mau General.

The mixture of emotion and trauma heightened my interest in Africa, an interest that I retain still today. I have travelled over much of 'the Dark Continent', from the equatorial rain forest of the Congo to the Kalahari Desert and from the summit of Kilimanjaro to the Okavango Delta. I have seen lions and wildebeest aplenty; as well as the rare sitatunga and the bongo. In addition I have seen whales, penguins and great white sharks, if not 'in' Africa, in the sea washing along its southern shores.

I have seen the peoples of Africa too; Bushmen, Masai, Batwa (a small people related to Pygmies), and at the coronation of the King of Swaziland, more Zulu warriors in their tribal dress (and undress) than appeared in the film 'Zulu'. Then there were the remaining pioneers of Africa, the writers and the adventurers that I had the good fortune to meet in person – Sir Laurens van der Post, Elspeth Huxley, George Adamson, and yes, Michaela Denis. As I write memories come rushing back – a huge buffalo stampede with flying dust and pounding hooves; a simultaneous 'mock charge' by two male Tsavo lions – clearly the ancestors of the Tsavo 'man-eaters'; and George Adamson surrounded by birds and animals that trusted him, like a latter-day St Francis of Assisi. It is incredible that, in the end, with huge bravery, George Adamson died in a hail of bullets as an action man of over eighty. One African original remains: Tony Fitzjohn who for years worked for George, providing the muscle power and vigour as the old man slowed and tired. Tony and his young family are now just across the Kenyan border in Tanzania, helping to restore the Mukamazi wildlife reserve, with projects for black rhino and wild dogs, and with a female elephant and a lioness that almost regard him as a friend. Now, because of all these things my interest in Africa has turned into a love for Africa and Kenya in particular.

My first visit to Africa was in 1976; my last was just after Christmas, and now my love is mixed with fear. Over the years I have shared my experiences with others; I have been one of many tourists in the Masai Mara, at the Ark and watching a leopard in Tsavo West. Kenya's economy over many years depended on its tourists – and so did its wildlife. If lions, leopards, cheetahs, wildebeest and impala are bringing in foreign currency and creating jobs their collective future will be secure. If that money and job creation falls away then the land will become the commodity and not the animals; that land – huge tracts of it – will be seen as just right for development; for cattle ranching, or in the case of the Masai Mara – growing wheat. In the First World, development does not stop for wildlife – look at the hideous funicular railway in the Scottish Highlands, as just one recent example, so why should we expect the Kenyans or the Tanzanians to adopt different, purer principles?

While Kenya had a flourishing tourism industry its wildlife was safe; after the infamous 9/11, tourism has plummeted, helped by absurd British and American 'travel advisories' urging people to stay away. In addition British Airways even stopped flights to Nairobi for a period. I flew by Kenya Airways, and felt as safe as I ever do when flying.

Once at Nairobi I then flew to Malindi on the coast, which is in the heart of Kenya's northern Muslim coast. Yes, there are Muslims and mosques, but I felt completely safe. The facts are simple; sit at home watching elephants on BBC 2 and sending the odd donation to an elephant charity and Kenya's wildlife will be doomed. Get out of your armchair and go with friends to visit some of Kenya's fantastic wildlife parks and Kenya's wildlife will have a future. The choice is as simple and as stark as that.

19

Vanishing Orchards

It seems strange writing about a new book by Gordon Beningfield in 2005, as he died on May 4th 1998 at the young age of 61. I remember the date clearly; my birthday is May 3rd and my little lurcher Bramble died on May 4th 1999 at the ripe old age of 17. Gordon was my closest friend and Bramble was my most remarkable dog – Gordon would not mind me writing about dogs while remembering him as he had a succession of wonderful deerhounds. At the time of his death he had gone to the other doggy extreme and had a feisty Border terrier, Ted. Ted still rules the roost with Gordon's widow Betty and every time I arrive he greets me like a long lost friend and shows all the characteristics of a puppy, not of a middle aged terrier beginning to become portly.

For me that time of loss around 1998 was intensified by losing a whole gaggle of people who had inspired or influenced me, including both my parents, Laurens van der

Post and Sir Jimmy Goldsmith. Indeed I bought a new pair of shiny black leather shoes that I called my 'funeral shoes'; fortunately I have not had to wear them recently and so it's back to trainers.

Gordon Beningfield was a most remarkable man. I believe that he was the most gifted artist of his generation. Ironically for a country artist he was born in the Pool of London where his father was a lighterman and he only became a countryman courtesy of a nasty little Nazi – one Adolf Hitler. Gordon became an evacuee in a small Hertfordshire village and the effect the move had on him is shown in his numerous books and pictures. It is a most peculiar reason for saying 'thank you Adolf'.

At school he was dyslexic; on leaving school he was regarded as being 'too thick' for national service – yet Gordon was one of the brightest people I have ever known and possessed that great and rare gift of seeing beauty and re-creating it in art. Through his art too he had another gift, that of turning art into conservation. Before the BBC lost its way on countryside programmes he appeared regularly on television; he became a self-taught expert on Thomas Hardy (becoming a great lover of rural Dorset in the process) and he was the artist who, in my view, for the first time turned butterfly illustration into art. One of his butterfly paintings, of a large blue, became a cover for the *Radio Times* and he also produced a series of outstanding butterfly stamps for the Royal Mail. His love and passion for the countryside showed in everything he did; he was a rarity – a man without an ego trying to share the things that pleased him and which he thought were important. I shared platforms with him on several occasions – the halls were always packed and the people loved him; they would ask him questions, buy his books, and simply say 'thank you'. I continue to speak up and down the country at a variety of venues, yet whenever I mention Gordon's name many people still smile and nod with remembered affection.

So how has Gordon managed to produce a book at this time – so many years after his death? When he died, Gordon had been working on three projects – one for America which he had just started, and two for this country which were well under way. The first on songbirds had some way to go; although he became famous through butterflies he loved all aspects of nature and was desperately worried about our loss of songbirds. Because of this, with Betty's help, we brought together some of his earlier bird paintings to produce *Beningfield's Vanishing Songbirds*, which I published myself in 2001.

This left a beautiful series of blossom and apple paintings, as well as a number of sepia sketches. The quality of the pictures was so fine that Betty and her daughters Sally and Sarah, wanted them to be seen by a wider audience; so *Beningfield's Orchards* was born. In addition to the paintings Gordon left for his project, we have scoured the country for more of his unpublished work – butterflies, birds, animals and flowers, to complete the book.

With traditional orchards under greater threat than ever before, the book could not have come at a more appropriate time and I am sure that the project would have met with Gordon's complete approval. He loved traditional orchards and his own small ancient orchard behind his house at Water End was a constant source of inspiration. Not only did his trees supply him with traditional plums, pears and apples (both eating and cooking) but it also attracted birds, animals (domestic and wild), flowers and butterflies. As summer turned towards apple-picking time his orchard became a jungle and anybody wanting fruit had to risk the stings and thorns of nettles, thistles and brambles; but the taste of the fruit was always worth the discomfort. His fruit eating went beyond stuffing his pockets, because, in Betty, he married a wonderful, traditional country cook and so the smell of fruit was transferred to the kitchen in the form of pies, tarts, jams and chutney. In the course of helping Betty produce the book I had the pleasure of sampling her sausage and apple casserole (a meal fit for a king) her apple pie and her apple cake. In an age when some new houses in London are being built without kitchens, we have included some of Betty's fruit recipes in the book to make those non-cooking people feel hungry. To make it worse for them, some of Gordon's paintings are of food – baked apple, apple tart, and docky – cheese, apple and new bread laid out on a spotted handkerchief. For those not accustomed to 'docky' this was the old mid-morning break on farms when the workers would stop for a short rest and a snack. It was called 'docky' as in the early days the farmers would then 'dock' money from their wages for the time lost. The 'grub' was carried in the 'docky bag' – today corrupted to 'doggy bag'.

With orchards under threat Gordon's pictures have never been more appropriate and from his delicate skill it is almost possible to smell the blossom and taste the fruit. He has included all the old favourite apples, Coxes, Russets, Worcesters, Laxtons and Bramleys. Part of the pleasure of helping Betty to write the book was to discover the history of some of apples. One of our most famous apples is the Bramley; it was first raised between 1809 and 1813 by a Miss Mary Ann Brailsford and planted in a garden in Southwell in Nottinghamshire. It did so well that it was admired by a nurseryman, Mr Henry Merryweather, in the middle of the 1800s, when the tree was in the garden of a local butcher, a Mr Bramley. Consequently the apple is not named after the person who planted it, or indeed after the person who spread its reputation, but after the local butcher, who by chance happened to have this first wonderful fruiting apple.

Not all the stories are good however – the supermarkets only like large apples (it helps them to sell more). The Cox is a naturally small apple and to increase the size to supermarket specifications, the growers have to pick nearly half the crop early – simply to throw it away – to enable the remaining apples to grow larger than usual. With the increase in size comes a marked loss of taste and many growers believe that the supermarkets will gradually phase out the wonderful Cox's Orange Pippin.

At such a prospect, Gordon would have been outraged, as I am. It is my hope that the beautiful paintings of *Beningfield's Orchards* will re-awaken people to the wonders and the beauty of traditional orchards. If it does then it will help keep the countryside alive – the countryside that Gordon Beningfield loved so much.

20

Blair's Thought Police – Again

———

Oh no, Blair's 'Thought Police' have struck again – I have been tried by a kangaroo court and found guilty. My crime? – telling the truth as I see it. So, after more than three decades as a District Councillor, who has been a Committee Chairman and represented South Cambridgeshire District Council at numerous conferences and meetings, I have apparently brought the Council 'into disrepute', I have been 'reckless' and shown a lack of 'respect' (the currently in-fashion politically correct word). As a result I have been banned from some meetings for three months; I have been ordered to apologise to a Councillor who had a meeting with a multi-million pound developer, and at the age of 62, just like Winston in George Orwell's *1984* I must be 're-trained'; '2+2 = 5', 'war is peace' and the Prime Minister is our leader and I love him.

The last time my free speech was threatened I was thrown into a Cambridge police cell and it was only through the support of *The Mail on Sunday* that we saw off a piece of pure politically correct nonsense. As a traditional countryman, all I said at a country fair in Gloucestershire was: 'If you are a black, vegetarian, Muslim, asylum-seeking, one-legged lesbian lorry driver, I want the same rights as you.' This, according to an un-named informer in Gloucestershire, was 'inciting racial hatred'. The Gloucestershire police then came all the way to Cambridgeshire and persuaded the local police to put me in a cell – quite illegally. What a state to be in; while few police are available for real crime, plenty seem to be available for 'thought crime' – and the country is now swarming with what can only be described as politically correct 'informers' – just like the old Soviet empire.

Now this new piece of politically correct nonsense has a named informer – the inaccurately named Ethical Standards Officer for the Standards Board for England, an overpaid quango set up by Blair. Up and down the country County Councillors, District Councillors and Parish Councillors are being hounded for 'thought crimes'. As a result they are either giving up, having breakdowns or paying vast legal fees to defend themselves. A colleague recently paid over a thousand pounds in legal fees to prove himself innocent against spurious and ridiculous accusations. He won, in a written disputation, but has no right to claim costs or compensation for the time and trauma spent defending himself.

My crime was considered to be so heinous that I was ordered to attend a 'public hearing'. The Standards Committee Hearing Panel consisting of three local worthies would try me, in the presence of a barrister from London representing the Standards Board for England. Still, after all these years, with a quaint but misplaced belief in British justice, I decided to defend myself, with the help of a friend. And what was my crime? At a committee meeting I had said: 'In my opinion the relationship between some councillors, some officers and some developers is far too close and therefore it seems to me that it could be interpreted as a form of corruption. Corruption is not just the transfer of money from one person to another but in my view corruption can also be seen in the form of relationships with people who make decisions or who have power.' Nothing startling or unknown in that then; but the Chairman, a Tory lady, instructed me to expand – against my wishes – so I added: 'As I understand it, Councillor Mrs Tweedledum (from a neighbouring village), has been to a soirée with a developer, who had wanted to get planning permission for a sports complex in the green belt. In my view this was entirely wrong and it seems to me that this can give members of the public a very bad impression of the way the council works.'

Shock horror – this highly qualified statement was out of order – the word 'soirée' was a crime, I had failed to treat her with 'respect'. Yes, she had been to a meeting about a development in the Green Belt, but it hadn't been a soirée, it had been tea and biscuits. The fact that I had been ordered to spill the beans was irrelevant.

The green belt to the south of Cambridge consists of several hundred acres. It is nearly all owned by Cambridge University, individual Cambridge colleges and a developer. If the green belt is breached its value becomes measured in hundreds of millions of pounds and just like the nearby Cambridgeshire gypsies, the Cambridge colleges do seem to believe that they have a right to do whatever they like with their own land. Oh dear, it didn't look good, the panel arrived: one of the panel was a Bursar of a Cambridge college, and it got worse – he was also an active athletics official, while I was Convenor of 'The Countryside Against the London Olympics', not through a dislike of sport, but through disliking the Government's attitude to the countryside.

After just ten minutes it was already clear that I had lost; my faith in justice had been misplaced again. As I interjected, the Chairman sighed and looked to the ceiling; his body language said it all. Seven and a half hours later it was confirmed – I had lost. Yes, seven and a half hours – I can only assume that barristers don't like meetings lasting twenty minutes.

It got worse still; after Mrs Tweedledum and the Council's own Legal Officer had appeared to give conflicting evidence the Chairman of the Panel announced that his other colleague – an elderly woman of the same vintage as Mrs Tweedledum – had just realised that they attended the same bridge class together. Was this Zimbabwe, or a scene from Monty Python? It was hard to tell. At that point the hearing should have been cancelled, but it went on – and on – and on – and on.

The Panel seemed uninterested in the fact that the incident occurred when members of the Council's Planning Committee were discussing a proposal in a Conservation Area, by the developer, one of the richest men in England, reportedly worth £135m. It seemed to me that leniency was being shown to his application, to substantially alter his ex 'squire's' house. Two hundred yards down the road an old marine commando in his eighties, who was wounded three times in the Second World War, was refused permission to put a small garage and bedroom onto his modest detached house because it was 'near' a conservation area. The old squire's house, in the 'middle' of the Conservation Area, was given permission for numerous changes including a six-foot high wall along one boundary, in total contradiction to the council's own policies – as I understand them.

What the panel was interested in was the word 'soirée' and the London barrister was allowed to go on and on; he clearly enjoys playing Scrabble. At one point I was so impressed at his inventiveness that I expected to see pigs flying into the sunset – instead I had visions of kangaroos hopping across the courtroom floor.

The overall issue was simple: should councillors be entertained at private meetings by developers or landowners whether at a soirée, a dinner, or tea and buns? I had been invited to the developer's parties in the past and declined to go; apparently a planning officer was invited to a cricket dinner and accepted. Even John Prescott, the Government minister in overall charge of planning, was invited to a University presentation about developing the green belt at the University's invitation two years ago. He accepted, and quite shockingly commented favourably on the scheme – before the planning process had even started! How's that for the Ethical Standards Officer? My position was more simple than John Prescott's – I don't do meetings with developers.

So, after my years on the District Council, the Panel hearing represented the most ridiculous farce I have ever seen in local government. It was an attack on free speech, an affront to democracy, and what was the cost? Most of the council tax payers I have met since are outraged and it is the Standards Board of England that has caused this outrage.

It almost goes without saying that the kangaroo court was held at the spanking new £17.5m offices of South Cambridgeshire District Council at the new settlement of Cambourne. To raise some of the money for the new building, the Council's two prime site offices actually in Cambridge were sold. One, within a stone's throw of the railway station, has now been absorbed into a £250m scheme to redevelop Cambridge's station area. It was bought at a snip, in my opinion, for £4.5m. And who bought it? The developer in question.

So in a world in which black = white, and Blair is a statesman, I was found guilty and must be punished. Lulu watched all this in total astonishment: 'Is that man (the Council's legal officer) really employed by the Council?' she asked incredulously. More to the point: 'You are not to apologise to that woman – Mrs Tweedledum.'

For the three members of the Panel, Tony Blair, and the Standards Board for England, I have just one short quote from Tacitus; it is about corruption: 'The more corrupt the state, the more numerous the laws'.

21

A Load of Bull

———

This chapter is something of a celebration – I am still alive and Alan, the raging Aberdeen Angus bull, has returned to his home. Thank you to all those people who wrote and rang – thank you as well to all those who sent horror stories of their own, from stroppy bulls to savage 'stag' turkeys. There were others, of course, who couldn't stop laughing at my discomfort – very unkind.

After my initial scares with Alan I only checked the cattle by vehicle. We wondered about using Lulu's little black Mercedes 'A' class – but on consideration we thought its colour and graceful lines might be too much for Alan – he might try and mate with it, with us inside. Instead, we approached cautiously in the tank-like 'Isuzu Trooper'. Alas it's back to Japanese after my British Freelander fell to pieces – but that's another story.

Several times Alan ran up to the Trooper snorting and shaking his head – if only the car had been fitted with a bull-bar – that is now on my Christmas list. Once I thought he was going to charge the side door – but he pulled back at the last minute. I don't know why he took such a dislike to me. Lulu wondered if we should play him classical music to calm him down – but alas the only tape we had was Status Quo, which made him worse.

Nor did he only terrorise me. Whenever a neighbour was training her young horse and Alan saw them he would stand at the fence roaring and pawing the ground. She thought that one strand of electric fence was not enough and quickly retreated every time. Then he would stand at the field gate challenging my farming neighbour's cattle across the road. Several young bullocks foolishly challenged him back, but fortunately the threat of electric shocks kept them apart.

With my old yokel friends Mick, Dave and Denis, we plotted. How would we get him back to the farm and into a trailer once his task of ravishing all my young lady cows had been completed? We drove the cattle back to the farm using the safety shield of the Trooper. With sticks being waved through the windows it was like a scene from 'Last of the Summer Wine'. Alan wandered into the covered yard – the cows stayed outside. 'Got you,' I shouted in triumph as I slammed the gate. He rumbled and swore and I thought he was going to jump. How would we get him into the trailer?

I was tense. He was still looking at me in a rather old-fashioned way. The trailer arrived – the stockman was Scottish. He backed up – I had my inhaler, mobile phone and stick at the ready – the twelve bore was in the Trooper. We opened the gates, 'Get in' said Jock, and Alan calmly walked into the trailer. 'Where's the fierce bull?' he asked. I looked skywards in embarrassment.

One odd feature of the Alan saga is the fact that when he was being driven to the farm in the first place, he and his owner were flagged down by the police in the company of a Trading Standards Officer. Alan's bull passport and travel documents were demanded and if they had not been produced there would have been a large fine. Fortunately all the paperwork was intact and Alan continued on his way.

Oddly though, there are instances in Cambridgeshire when other travellers have no papers and nobody seems concerned. A friend was driving through the Fens when he saw a deeply tanned, lightly clothed gentleman, walking along the roadside in a thunderstorm. He picked him up and found that he could speak no English. Using sign language, and talking slowly and loudly, in the English way, he gained the impression that the wet wanderer had no idea where he was or where he was going. Worried about his passenger's welfare he took him to the nearby reception centre for asylum seekers and illegal immigrants. 'Have you got papers for him sir?' a uniformed official asked. 'No.' 'Then we can't take him. See if the police will take him.' He went three steps up the chain of command – all with the same response. 'But surely it's your job to get him papers – I was just doing him a favour.' 'That's no concern of ours sir.'

The visitor's mobile phone rang. Somebody in broken English asked that the gentleman be dropped off in Tesco's car park so that he could be picked up and taken to London. Sure enough, as soon as they arrived at the Tesco car park, the wet visitor was whisked away by more dusky gentlemen. That evening on the news it was said that five illegal immigrants from Bulgaria had jumped from a container lorry. Four had been captured and one was still missing.

So, if you are an Aberdeen Angus bull in Britain with no papers, you are in big trouble. If you are a Bulgarian illegal immigrant and presented to the immigration service with no papers, officialdom doesn't want to know. What a load of bull!

22

Living with Foxes

———

It is incredible that for years the most important political issue in Britain has been foxes. Yes, foxes: should people on horses or on foot be free to chase foxes, or should foxes be free to chase whatever they like?

My problem here is that I love foxes, so how can I be objective? They have always intrigued me and they are one of the most fascinating and beautiful animals to be found in Britain. I have got up at the crack of dawn to watch fox cubs playing outside their earth (the hole where foxes live) in Haley wood, one of the oldest and muddiest woods in East Anglia. I have crawled on my stomach to get a better view; I have been so close to wild foxes that I could have touched them; on one occasion a vixen squatted down to relieve herself practically on my foot; she looked up and saw me almost in disbelief, before rushing off in panic.

Believe it or not I have seen foxes swimming across the little brook at the southern edge of the farm, one doing a bellyflop as it jumped in to get away from my dogs; I have seen them up trees, particularly old willows, that have many holes and passageways in which to hide and I have even come across them sunbathing on a large branch many feet from the ground. We have had them on the roofs of some of our farm buildings and I suspect during the winter they regularly snuggle up in the hay.

I have seen them stalking pheasants, and to see a cock

pheasant minus its tail is usually a sign of a narrow escape. I have watched them chasing rabbits, and as a small farmer I have seen them making off with some of my hens. I have heard stories of foxes rolling and dancing until fascinated birds have come close enough to be caught. Roosting pheasants have certainly disappeared, leaving behind just a pile of feathers, giving credence to the story of foxes walking round and round a tree until any roosting pheasant falls down through dizziness. In addition I have cuddled them, fed them and played with them, as I have had a number of semi-tame foxes that were simply wonderful friends as well as pets. Inevitably, as with all wild animals kept in captivity, some met with very sticky ends and when this happened I cried bucketsful of tears, and my world temporarily fell apart.

My fascination with foxes started as a child on our small Cambridgeshire farm where I still live, and where a fox took one of our large geese just ten days ago. Not only did my introduction to foxes come from stories of foxes stealing the

hens – and in seeing a number of headless hens outside the henhouse after one daytime visit – but I was also introduced to the foxes of literature and children's storybooks. There were those wonderful stories of Chicken Licken, The Sly Fox and The Little Red Hen, Brer Rabbit outwitting Brer Fox, and the lovable three little foxes created by A. A. Milne in *When We Were Very Young*. Later they were joined by that master storyteller Roald Dahl's creation *The Fantastic Mr Fox*. Then came the fox in real literature *Wild Lone* by 'BB', (the pen name of Denys Watkins-Pitchford) and that remarkable, descriptive and breathless poem by John Masefield, *Reynard the Fox*.

There was only one thing missing from all these stories of foxes – an encounter with a real live fox. Today this seems amazing with almost as many foxes living in the towns as in the country, but when I was a boy, and then a teenager, foxes were scarce and seldom seen.

The reasons for this are obvious, or should be, to all those over fifty. When I attended my local infant school in the late 1940s I had to pass through the village High Street. Many of the houses, both private and council, had back-garden hens. Today they would be called 'free range' and were kept in a shed at the bottom of the garden to supply eggs to help the family budget. During the day they would range over the whole garden or were allowed to scrap in their own run and at night they were shut up. If a fox appeared and a hen or even the entire residents of a henhouse were slaughtered, guns, snares and the then legal gin trap appeared and any marauding fox paid a heavy price.

In addition, at that time rabbits were rampant and bred – like rabbits. They were totally out of control and did enormous damage to crops and grazing meadows. As a result, before myxomatosis ('mexy') struck – that cruel disease developed by scientists and approved by politicians – rabbits were so numerous that there were several full-time, professional rabbit-trappers, and wild rabbit was a popular and regular addition to the dinner table. When a fox visited the snare line before the trappers, and their incomes were threatened, then guns, snares and gin traps again overcame the problem.

Then came 'mexy', the rabbit population was decimated and rabbit-trappers, one of the fox's worst predators, went out of business. The gin trap was outlawed on cruelty grounds, and that coincided with another great change suiting the fox – supermarkets. With the arrival of cheap eggs in supermarkets, regardless of the way in which the eggs had been produced, the backyard hen became doomed. It was quicker, cleaner and more convenient to buy cheap eggs from the shop than to feed hens at the bottom of the garden. The fact that supermarket eggs were produced by hens kept in battery cages, or that fowl for eating were intensively reared were of no concern to the average shopper – out of sight out of mind.

So the major pressures on the fox were removed and the populations in both country and town rocketed. As a result there are now possibly more foxes in Britain than ever before. Their only natural predators (apart from Man) the wolf and the brown bear were exterminated years ago, and apart from the odd few taken by golden eagles, domestic dogs are the only other concern. What has made life even easier is the fact that so many people now have overflowing bird tables throughout the winter and our roads have become a sort of McDonald's take-away for foxes, providing a never ending supply of fresh, squashed high-protein meat in the form of hedgehogs, pheasants, blackbirds, muntjac deer and even flattened household cats. I have found a dead road casualty cat outside a fox's earth and there is growing evidence that perfectly healthy cats are also being taken. Consequently the average fox is well fed, and hunting gardens for bread, and roadside edges for meat keeps them full and healthy during the winter, when historically it was a time of hunger and high mortality.

Because of all these circumstances I did not see a real, live fox until I was well into my teens. Now it is most unusual if I don't see or smell a fox while walking my few fields (fox's urine has a very distinctive and pungent smell). In addition I have had several foxes as pets. My first, Cassius, I found as a newborn cub in a hole in a tree, at least ten feet from the ground. He was so young that he still had his eyes shut and I had to rush into Cambridge to buy a doll's feeding bottle to give him milk. He grew into a wonderful and beautiful dog fox and had Rinty, a Labrador puppy, as company. They played for hours together in the garden; the Labrador pup grew much larger than the fox but Cassius was more agile, turning on a sixpence, and when actually engaged in a mock fight the fox's brush was always between him and the Labrador's jaws. This did have one advantage; whenever Cassius decided to wander off on his own and refuse to come back, Rinty would always catch him by the tail and hold him until he was retrieved.

Because Cassius would chase anything that moved he had to be put into a run whenever there was nobody present to supervise play. Even so he managed to kill a hedgehog and a blackbird that went into his run and he would snap his jaws shut on passing bumblebees and swallow them with relish.

In the house he would jump onto the sideboard from a standing start without knocking anything over and he would steal and crack hazelnuts expertly. He loved chocolate and chocolate cake. Although a delight indoors he would not be house-trained, often leaving the living room smelling like a fox's earth. Similarly he would not walk to a lead without pulling, and foxes certainly cannot be domesticated like a dog which explains why all the photographs of 'pet' foxes show the owners holding them fast around the neck.

On his first escape, he rushed up to one of our free-range hens and caught it by the tail. Heaving mightily, he was left sprawling in a heap when all the feathers suddenly came out The next time he made no such mistake and he bit me as I tried to retrieve the dead hen. On his last venture out he was shot and I cried a bucketful of tears; although brought up as a pet – he returned to the wild – that is where he wanted to be.

The end of my second fox cub was much quicker. A woman from a neighbouring village found a tiny cub wandering in the road, wet and cold. It had probably been dropped by its mother as she had been carrying it to a fresh earth. Fearing for its safety the lady brought it to me and with a warm box by the Aga and the doll's feeding bottle back in use it made good progress. Sadly the progress was too good; for when Rinty was chewing on a new bone the cub tried to steal a bit of meat. With one chop the cub was left dead in a growing pool of its own blood and again tears flowed. It was not the dog's fault; the cub's ambition had just been unexpected.

Sidney was another superb dog fox and one day he simply disappeared. Usually my foxes would return after a day or two of freedom, but Sidney vanished and I assumed that was that. Several months later we began having 'fox trouble'. Nearly every night the hens would wake us shrieking hysterically, some nights break-ins would occur and there would be dead and dying hens. One night Rinty cornered the hen thief under the henhouse and I ran for the gun. I aimed at the fox with the spotlight on him and just as I was about to pull the trigger it moved – it was wearing a blue collar – it was Sidney. I let him go and never saw him again – I also wrote a cheque out to my father for all the dead hens.

My last fox, Rusty, was a small vixen. I took her on after she had outgrown the small town flat where a friend had kept her as a cub. She too was wonderful. She would jump onto my shoulders and rub her chin through my hair. One day it all went suddenly warm and wet – she had peed on my head – I had become her territorial marking post. The shampoo came out in record time in case the local foxhounds went past.

A friend in a neighbouring village also had a male pet fox called Botoch and in January (the mating season for foxes) we tried to get them to breed. After much swearing at one another they settled down but their relationship never developed into cubs.

In the summer she would dig great holes in her run, and inevitably she would escape. Her first spell of freedom lasted over a day and she returned suddenly squealing and wagging her brush (foxes have a wide range of noises). As she got older she would stay away longer. Each time she went I would walk along the hedgerows with the dogs, calling her name, but she never returned until she wanted to. She returned one night quite unexpectedly; it was bright and moonlit and I was checking the cattle yard at 11.00pm. Suddenly she was at my feet whining and wagging her brush before rolling over to have her stomach rubbed. On another occasion she was away for four or five days and I had given up all hope of ever seeing her again. On that excursion she emerged from thick brambles in the brook meadows and greeted the dogs like long lost friends before running over to me. She was in good condition and had obviously been feeding well.

Her final escape came in 1979. My political life was not very advanced at the time and I was a Conservative, absurdly standing for parliament in Bethnal Green. Nevertheless with the election campaign in full flow I took several days off to return home to search for her. We found her eventually almost unmarked but with her neck broken – almost certainly killed by a large dog, as most dogs seem to have a real antipathy to foxes. As usual I cried a bucketful of tears – wild pets and tears seem to go hand in hand; I would never have another pet fox, preferring them to take their chance in the wild and hoping that they would meet hounds and not a snare or a gun.

My encounters with wild foxes have been numerous. I have had young cubs come out of an old earth and actually play around my feet and on one occasion a full-grown fox collided with me as it was fleeing from my little lurcher Bramble. Encounters in the farmyard have been less pleasant. Over the years they have taken hundreds of hens and cleared us out of ducks and guinea fowl. Several fully grown geese have also bitten the dust – one in broad daylight. Of course clever people say: 'You should shut your hens up.' In the next breath they say: 'We only buy free-range eggs'. To which I reply: 'Oh free-range hens – you mean hens that are not shut up?'

Not only do foxes feed on farmyard hens, but they also like wild birds, many of them protected – from lapwings and grey partridges, to avocets and stone curlews. Sadly a fox will not just kill one bird, but as many as it can get its jaws onto and whole colonies of ground-nesting terns have been decimated by foxes. As a result I do not know one serious conservation body that does not control foxes.

Because of my close association with foxes many people assume that I am against fox hunting. I am not and it is my view that the hunting ban is a serious mistake. A hunted fox is killed, or it gets away; the other methods of fox control are far crueller and leave many animals maimed and injured – so the ban will actually increase fox suffering. Then, of course, society actually tolerates activities that are far crueller than hunting – Muslim halal slaughter, broiler fowl sold in supermarkets and the production of soya beans – yes, soya beans. Last year an area the size of Wales was lost in the

Amazon basin, for additional soya bean cultivation – to be fed to cattle and affluent Western vegetarians. That involves not foxes, but a whole eco-system being destroyed, yet most people seem uninterested. Then there is the issue of individual freedom and democracy – after all, that is what we are supposed to be fighting for in Iraq. It is odd too isn't it that our Prime Minister – Bomber Blair – seems to believe that bombing Arabs is far more acceptable than chasing a fox – how bizarre is that?

23

Transformed Grumpy Old Man

I can hardly believe it; marriage? Doesn't time fly when you are enjoying yourself! It has been an astonishing learning curve for me since I placed the engagement ring as romantically as I could on Anita's finger; we were in an ancient wood, leaning against a giant oak tree. Unfortunately the wood is situated next to a maggot factory; the wind was coming from the wrong direction and the smell was disgusting – but it seemed like a good idea at the time. Incidentally, I had better explain – Anita's nickname is 'Lulu'; I most certainly have not been chasing two women around as scurrilously suggested by some. Yes – I was kissed by my bridesmaid rather passionately, but sadly I haven't seen Corset since she returned to the Cambridgeshire Foxhounds, where she will hunt entirely within the law. Foxhounds are like that – they are far more law abiding than all those hundreds of thousands of car drivers who ignore the 70mph speed limit on motorways and use their mobile phones at the same time.

For an old bachelor of 61 the most amazing change came about in the living room where a carpet suddenly appeared and a strange electronic contraption called a 'Hoover' was used to attack it. This led to a friend looking on the scene in amazement: 'Robin, this just doesn't look like your house any more', he said, before seizing a large pile of papers and throwing them all over the floor. The other large change is in the refrigerator. Previously it contained nothing but a few pieces of cheese, as if I was conducting an experiment into growing mould in a cold climate, and a few well past their 'sell-by dates' yogurts – the question being whether I would eat them before they exploded. Now the fridge is full of fresh edible food – it is astonishing. After getting up early during lambing, there was Anita to greet me: 'Would you like some tea? Would you like an egg?'

That is one of the downsides of marriage – Anita is a wonderful cook. Normally at this time of year I lose weight – but now I am putting it on and when I stand upright I can no longer see my feet. We have had a language problem too. Being an ordinary old country boy I have 'dinner' at dinner time (1pm) and suppertime. The posh Anita has 'lunch' and 'dinner'. The bonus in all this however is that Anita is one of the few people I know who is not 'toothist' and she has no problem with me not wearing my false teeth. It means that if I get any tough meat or hard peas I just have to suck extra hard.

She has also insisted that I bath and shower more, regardless of East Anglia's growing water crisis. Previously I bathed twice a year, on the longest day and the shortest day; now she insists that I bath every time we go out – it has meant that I have had to find somewhere else to keep the bike. Similarly I only have to leave my clothes on the floor for five minutes and they are gone – into the washing machine – again wasting gallons of water. Underpants, jeans, the lot – they're getting washing fatigue and my jeans have shrunk to such an extent they could seriously damage my health. Why can't she wash my underpants once a fortnight, like in the good old days?

But Lulu's washing has caused me a problem too; suddenly there on my washing line was a row of scrumcaps and I didn't even know she played rugby. They turned out to be items of clothing called 'thongs' that most elderly gentlemen like me know nothing about. When they are worn out they will never make good lamb blankets or dusters like my old grandmother's silk bloomers. As for 'exfoliation' I still don't know what that means.

As far as I have discovered Lulu only has one fault – she is a terrible navigator. As a recent report indicated, homosexuals and women find it difficult to read maps. Hence she knows the difference between right and wrong, but not left and right. She is to navigation what John Prescott is to anorexia. The other day when we were supposed to be going west to Chipping Norton I found myself being driven north up the A1.

So quite contrary to all those people who warned me against it, I am finding married life an extremely happy experience. There is only one word in Anita's vocabulary that I don't understand and I am not going to find out. It sounds slightly threatening and contains three letters; she keeps referring to something strange called an AGA.

24

Dedicated Follower of Fashion

Incredible, last week saw me married, nine months to the day. Odd things have happened during that time – Anita (Lulu) my gorgeous wife is a good cook, and so, instead of her waist line expanding in the traditional manner – it is mine that has expanded at such a rate that people look at me as if my waters are about to burst. Hence, being a keen follower of fashion, the trousers I wear these days are a very modest little number from Marks and Spencer's with a rather attractive elasticated waist. Anything else would require braces, as a belt would cut off the supply of blood to my legs.

Fashion has supplied me with one important surprise since my wedding day. I have learnt that if I go to a country show, or a point-to-point to leave my Visa card behind, as Lulu always sees something attractive; a new top by Burberry, Joules or Weird Fish – or a coat from Musto or Barber. All I have to say is: 'Oh no! I've forgotten my card' and she buys it herself – what a perfect relationship.

To become more acquainted with what Lulu ought to be wearing I decided to go to the London Fashion Week – last week. 'Don't you go near any models and start snorting coke', she ordered – apparently that is what can happen in sinful London. 'No', I replied, 'I'll take my normal drugs for a visit to the big city – soluble aspirin, Rennies and of course Imodium.' Snorting Imodium – what a thought!

And what should I wear for one of Europe's leading fashion shows? I decided I would go in what I usually wear at The Hoops on darts night – I call it the Rural Retro Look. Underneath my elasticated trousers I wore my usual Y-fronts from Marks and Spencer's. On one occasion in London I found I had got them on back to front: 'Make sure you've got them on the right way round this time', Lulu advised. 'You know what that London fashion lot are like.' Then there were odd socks – I just grab whatever comes to hand – I understand that this is the height of fashion. On this occasion I had one yellow and blue – the other was red and featured large-uddered cows. Then a rather battered pair of trainers; an attractive 'Barmy Army' polo shirt to celebrate England's great cricket victory; a skull and cross bones bandana – very 'cool' – and last but not least an attractive corduroy tunic from John Brocklehurst, the 'Gentlemen's Outfitter' of Bakewell. I had wanted to wear my wonderful silk waistcoat covered in hand-painted sheep – but sadly I had left it hanging in a wardrobe in Derbyshire the week before. Oh – and of course – I had to wash my hair with the shampoo that has kept my mop so clean and curly for all these years – Vosene – it ought to be the height of fashion but unfortunately I'm told by Lulu that it smells like essence of rodent.

Oh dear, what a culture shock. Is fashion really that important? Surely it is just that – 'fashion' – transitory, super-ficial, unreal – so why the hundreds of press photographers and dozens of camera crews for something that is simply passing by? And what a venue – the Natural History Mus-eum; there was certainly much natural history to view with a great deal of preening, displaying and marking of territories; people being seen, wanting to be seen and hanging on.

I was ushered to the catwalk – what a waste of space. It would have made a fantastic indoor cricket pitch. The lights blazed, rock music pounded and the creations came – by John

Rocha of Ireland. To me the dresses appeared to have been made from an undertaker's off-cuts – black – and often see-through – I don't think these 'nipple flashers' would be for Lulu in The Hoops – she would be causing some of the regulars spluttering, or even drowning in their beer. Journalists and buyers were busy making sketches and notes – oddly, many were chewing in good football manager fashion – yes – gum chewing with mouth open appears to have become a fashion accessory; the bank of two hundred photographers were flashing away – it was unreal. And the models? How are their arms attached to their bodies? They appear to have no shoulders. How on earth do such spindly shoulders work the Hoover and peel the potatoes? I suppose the most strenuous exercise some undertake in the course of a week is to hand the cheque over to the bank cashier. Would they be able to lift a set of darts on darts night I wondered? Several of them looked as if they needed the post-darts pizzas and sandwiches. Perhaps there ought to be a new character in Little Britain – 'Angeline the Anorexic Model'. They were nearly all taller than me by a foot, and one, Barbara Di Creddo, had arrived from Brazil especially for the occasion.

I suppose my eyes were just being unsophisticated – according to the blurb:

'The Summer Collection is defined by a true tenderness set against beautifully sculpted modern forms – to create a silhouette that is light but essentially resolute.

A palette of broken white, yellow, coral and violet suffuse the collection with an innocent freshness, against the calm strength and intensity of black, steel and slate.

Texture and fabric are as ever important: crushed luster cottons and poplins, cool wool (how can wool be cool – it is made to keep sheep warm), sparkled linen

and brocades are softened with silk chiffons,
georgettes, taffetas and guipure lace'

– silly me – I should have known.

Outside I was surrounded by a bevy of 'Sugar Babes' promoting a new scent – they had slogans printed across their ample Page Three chests – I had to wear my glasses to bring it all into focus – they seemed impressed with my 'Essence of Rodent'.

There were stands selling to 'the trade' – jewellery, hats, shoes, bags – I tried to buy Lulu a hat from 'Fred Bare' – but sadly they had to be ordered in bulk. It was odd – there were items in feather, pearl, shell and leather – all bits of dead creatures – so why do some find fur so abhorrent? I don't understand. Suddenly there was a familiar name – 'Lulu' – it was Lulu Guinness who was selling some attractive bags – some bearing appropriate quotes: 'You can be too Rich – and too Thin', and 'Beauty comes from the Heart – Not from a Jar'. At an underwear stand 'Yes Master', an effeminate gentleman was saying 'Oh, yellow and purple go so well together'. I think not – but then I'm only an old rustic.

At the soya drink stand another was announcing: 'Oh, you must come up and see the new cottage in Norfolk – we'll be laying the new garden in three weeks – and we're going to Mexico for the new year.' Needless to say soya also seems to be a growing fashion; at the London Fashion Show it was being touted as the 'Official Wellbeing Drink to London Fashion Week'; it 'Lowers Cholesterol', but if it 'lowers Cholesterol', being shipped in from China or Brazil it also 'raises Global Warming' while destroying acres of Brazilian forest. Never mind, it does 'Lower Cholesterol'.

The newspapers were full of Fashion Week's snorting and cavorting and so I entered the toilets sideways – ready for a quick getaway. Inside I stood next to a gentleman wearing a

T-shirt proclaiming: 'Don't Worry I'm not Gay'. There were no signs of white powder around and as my Y-fronts were the right way round I did not panic. Mission accomplished I reversed out – only to back into a gentleman wearing a dress. I don't think that would go down well at The Hoops.

A poster proclaimed 'Gypsy Chick' – that was odd too; around my small farm in Cambridgeshire, with illegal travellers camps and light fingers, 'gypsy' is not a polite word, nor is the fact appreciated that the BBC's Comic Relief has given money to traveller groups to help with 'basic rights' and legal advice. That is what many of us in the country feel we have lost, 'basic rights' and we certainly need legal advice to help deal with illegal travellers. In London, however, things are different, with flowing 'gypsy' skirts being the latest fashion.

Gypsies, Turkish gypsies and peasants by Bora Aksu also inspired the next show on the catwalk. Why do models walk as they do – not only are they thin with minimal shoulders but most have thin legs too. Poor Lulu thinks she has knobbly knees; I can assure her that she is not alone. As they walk they place one foot exactly in front of the other, lifting their knees unusually high. If I had a cow walk like that I would call the vet immediately; perhaps one or two had been snorting Imodium after all. Then as they slow in front of the cameras they lean backwards – their skin pale and heavily made up – I found the whole thing bizarre. I would like to see clothes on girls with ruddy cheeks, real shoulders, a natural walk and who smile at the cameras. It really is 'fashion' – nothing to do with reality. A whole industry based on fantasy, with the money to go with it.

Behind the scenes before another show it was worse than the cattle sheds at the Royal Show; bodies, half naked, nearly naked and completely naked (that would have finished them off in The Hoops) changing clothes during rehearsals.

There were make-up artists with more brushes than the average painter and decorator, and hairdressers with a variety of fearsome looking implements for curling and straightening hair.

The final show was greeted with sirens and planes – it sounded like war. I sat next to a Swedish writer wearing a 'Biggles' flying helmet and some sort of fur drape. She said: 'It was a dead fox once.' Across the way were a crowd of enthusiastic Japanese – it must have reminded them of Pearl Harbour. The work of Robert Cary-Williams, it said: 'continues to be inspired by the military and sees the combination of 1950's structure and drama playing inspiration to this latest offering from London Fashion week's quintessentially English designer'. What an incredible selection of 'new' clothes. The men were wearing shorts and shirts similar to the ones I have been wearing around the farm all summer and which Lulu has been trying to get me to bin. Surely this must make me a fashion icon, ahead of my time – the only real difference was that the stains on my trainers are from genuine cowpats.

The dresses to me looked like bits and pieces of old sacking and fishnet picked up from a farmyard or old fishing quay. The models had to walk over a collection of panelled doors – giving them a rather precarious farmyard gait and several wore wire mesh around their posteriors as part of the dress. One was so crafted that it would have held ferrets – instead it held stuffed sparrows and a few other moth-eaten birds. I thought it was more an entry for the Turner Prize than a serious dress. How do you sit down if your backside is covered with wire-mesh and your left lower cheek is home to a perching dead sparrow? Come on! As John McEnroe said once: 'You cannot be serious'. The show ended for the day and I went briefly to the Natural History Museum for a bit of relief – there, near the main door, was the skeleton of a Moa

– a now extinct land bird from New Zealand. I'm sure it had better knees than some of the models.

With relief it was back in the real world. Lulu met me off the train. 'Did you get me a suitable present from London Fashion Week' she asked. She was in luck – I had got her a can of Diet Coke costing 70p. When I got home a friend phoned: 'Can I bring the ferrets over next week?' he said. 'Yes', I replied, 'as long as you keep them down your trousers and you're not wearing a dress.'

25

A Farming Manifesto

Two thousand and five was a remarkable year, with farming still in steep decline, and farm incomes averaging just £11,000 a year – a figure that most politicians wouldn't get out of bed for; the plight of British agriculture went almost unnoticed. At the general election – in which I participated and comfortably lost my deposit – the main parties (and the electorate) were uninterested, and that malaise washed over into the party conferences. Of course Tony Blair has taken up the mantra; 'Scrap the CAP! Scrap the CAP!', a beautiful refrain that he sang in duet with Bob Geldof at the G8 celebrations for inflated egos. In fact most of what was said at the time about saving Third World farmers was an apology for raw globalisation, which if realised would drive 1.5 billion Third World farmers off the land and throw them into the expanding shanty towns of Africa, Asia and Latin America.'Make Poverty History'? I don't think so; and what about the rural poverty in Britain, among our traditional family farmers? Not only does the present Government ignore the problem – it helped to create it.

Way back in 1993, with help from *The Daily Telegraph*, I, with a few friends, launched The Countryside Restoration Trust. Our concern was the destruction of wildlife on farmland through intensive methods of production. In my view we have led the way in environmentally friendly farming. On our Cambridgeshire farm we have all the wildlife (except the lapwing) that the Government claims it wants to get back, although of course no Government Minister will visit us – we are too politically incorrect – or honest – according to taste. We have barn owls, brown hares, otters, cowslips, marbled white butterflies and so on. We have achieved what we set out to achieve.

We have now moved on. Yes, we still want wildlife – but we regard the farmer and the farm worker as endangered as our wildlife and so we want wildlife friendly farming, but

farming that will also make a profit for the farmer and his family and produce quality and seasonal food. I suppose that separates us from other farming bodies and charities. Our three farms have resident farmers farming them; on the RSPB's 'Hope Farm', for instance, the farmhouse is empty – producing skylarks and no livelihood or lifestyle – quite extraordinary. If I wasn't a member of the RSPB I would be tempted to call it 'Hopeless Farm'.

Zac Goldsmith is one of the CRT's newest Trustees and before his recent elevation to a Tory environmental think-tank with St John Selwyn Gummer, I sat down with Zac and on the back of an envelope we hatched a farming manifesto that would transform the countryside and British farming. It took us ten minutes, yet the Government – and the Tory Government before it – finds farming difficult.

Here it is:

1. Break the armlock of the supermarkets (as Blair promised years ago before he went off bombing Arabs). New taxes on supermarket food should be introduced based on the air miles and road miles of their stock. Supermarket car park spaces should be taxed so making supermarkets more environmentally responsible and making competition more equal. (Blair's original farming Guru was of course Lord Christopher Haskins – a major supplier to the supermarkets through his companies Northern Foods and Express Dairies).

2. There should be a tax on aviation fuel for freight in an attempt to make the competition between 'local' and 'global' more equal. (Somehow Blair and Geldof seem unable to realise that some Third World producers are getting their produce into British supermarkets at a cheaper price than growers in Britain. At Tesco's – which

I visit regularly, to be annoyed and not to buy – Zimbabwean peas and beans are for sale. So as half the country goes short of food, Zimbabwe exports food to Tesco's – how immoral is that?).

3. Every imported carcass of meat – from Thai chicken to Argentinean beef – should have a passport as detailed as a British cattle passport, to show all movements from the point of origin. They should also be required to adopt the same welfare standards as British farmers.

4. There should be a policy of local food procurement, where possible, imposed on local authorities, schools and universities, the civil service, the military, hospitals and prisons.

5. There should be two-tier regulations allowing local food to have less stringent regulations than food travelling thousands of miles. The aim should be 'relax locally' – 'tighten globally'. It is common sense that hygiene rules involving produce travelling for hours through hot climates should be tighter than food produced and sold locally. Yet absurdly, British food often has greater regulation than food imported from Thailand and China. (This would also encourage the re-emergence of local slaughterhouses in Britain. And who started their demise under absurd European red tape? Why, John Major's Tory Government. And who in particular was responsible, as Secretary of State for Agriculture? Sorry Zac – it was none other than John Seldom Glummer).

6. Re-instate the Milk Marketing Board to ensure a return to fair, humane, cow friendly and wildlife friendly milk production. (Astonishingly the ruination of dairy farming was again achieved under the Tories with the destruction

of the MMB. To stay in business most dairy farmers still operating have had to intensify – cutting grass for silage in some instances from March to November. Consequently intensive dairy farming has created a wildlife desert – destroying the nests of lapwings, curlews, skylarks etc and chopping up the young of hares and roe deer. Ironically, the RSPB also bought a dairy farm on Islay several years ago. Instead of leading the way in wildlife friendly dairy farming, it immediately, incredibly, sold the dairy cows. At great financial risk the CRT hopes to take on a dairy farm in the near future in the hope of developing a wildlife/farmer/cow friendly way producing milk).

7. Deficiency payments should be the chosen method of subsidy, linked to sustainable and wildlife friendly methods of production. There should be a built-in upper limit – to prevent the creation of 'subsidy millionaires'. In a year of good market prices there would be little subsidy to pay. In a year of low prices there would be more subsidy to pay. With the armlock of the supermarkets broken, fairer market prices would result and the subsidies paid would be lower anyway. The system would be simple and straightforward – not like the new and absurd bureaucratic nightmare 'The Single Farm payment'.

8. Of course this simple and common sense manifesto would not be allowed under the Common Agricultural Policy, which means just one thing – Britain should leave the CAP.

How easy is all that?

To show how British agricultural policy makers are totally out of touch with reality, DEFRA recently sent a pamphlet to every farmer in England – *Farm Business Advice Service – Knowing your options*. One of the untitled pictures is strange;

-it turns out to be of the soya bean harvest in Germany. That could be the subliminal message to British farmers – if you want to get on and be appreciated, move to Germany – that could be your best option!

26

What a Hoot

Owls have never been more popular: thanks to Harry Potter cuddly owls, owl tea cloths, and even owl curtain designs are the presents that both children and adults want. The only trouble is that the cuddly owl is now far more common than the real owl – the tawny owl hooting in the old church yard and the ghostly barn owl quartering the water meadows at dusk have almost become more fictitious than Harry Potter.

It is another of those rural disasters that our politicians, both local and national, seem oblivious to. At one time the owl was one of our most noticeable birds, hooting or screeching at night and flying by on silent wings. In folklore they were not just associated with wisdom, but also witchcraft and if an owl flew into a house it was said to be an omen of death. Witches themselves were very keen on owls as an ingredient for their various brews and inevitably Shakespeare had the witches in Macbeth including an 'owlet's wing' in their ominous potion. The reason why owls were linked to witchcraft was simply because they were associated with darkness and night. The reasons why they were plentiful were also obvious – in the days before combine harvesters, stacks of wheat, barley and oats would be standing in the farmyards for months on end, attracting rats and mice, and they in turn brought in owls wanting supper. In the fields, hedgerows and spinneys there was also undergrowth with plenty of wild seeds, fruit and nuts – just right for rodents and so the menu of the owl spread from farmyard to distant field, and rat, mouse, vole and even the beautiful harvest mouse all helped to keep a healthy owl population in food.

When I was boy owls were commonplace. At night every other telegraph pole seemed to be a perching place for a little owl – whose diet also included beetles. In the summer with young to feed they would sometimes hunt during the day too and their presence would often be betrayed by songbirds scolding them, with blackbirds, thrushes, sparrows and robins all warning of this occasional bird eater and dive-bombing it to try and move it on.

If a tawny owl was found trying to get some daytime sleep, half concealed in ivy, it would get the same treatment and determined bombing runs by cock blackbirds would often drive it away. In fact rescuing a tawny owlet that had fallen out of its nest is one of my best (and worst) memories of childhood. A neighbour found the tawny owl chick at the base of a tree where it had obviously fallen out of its nest. As we went to save it from dogs and cats it clicked its beak at us in anger. Soon we had it in a cage and with help from a friend who worked in a medical laboratory, we fed Socrates with a steady supply of white mice and he soon became tame. Whenever mice were not available, we would shoot sparrows, or even give him small pieces of beef wrapped in hen feathers. The feathers were to provide 'roughage', as healthy owls make pellets of indigestible bones, fur and feathers and eject them. Finding a pellet often shows where an owl is perching and dissecting the pellet will reveal its diet.

Socrates was a beautiful bird and developed the incredible plumage of an adult tawny – soft, almost fragile feathers of an amazing number of delicate browns and duns. His eyes were large and brown and he could swivel his head 180 degrees with absolutely no trouble. At times when he was perching on a chair or in the rose bushes it was difficult to tell which way he was supposed to be facing.

As is so often the case with animals and birds taken in from the wild his end was sad and the whole family shed many tears. We were so pleased with the way that he had grown into adulthood that we wanted to give him back his freedom. We simply let him go, without any experience of hunting live mice, hoping that he would come back for feeding if he became hungry. Instead he just perched at the top of a high elm, out of reach and slowly starved to death. By the time he came lower it was too late and his bright eyes dulled – it still fills me with sadness as I recall it.

Barn owls were the other common owls; white ghosts hunting through the mist at dusk and performing aerial acrobatics as they stalled, aimed and fell on furred movement below – the most amazing and beautiful hunters – for that is what every owl is, a hunter.

It seemed as if the world of the owl would never change – but it did. Dieldrin and DDT – toxic chemicals to protect seed corn – poisoned the rats, mice and birds that fed on the newly sown fields, and in turn poisoned the owls that fed on them. Disaster and extinction loomed, and a tragedy was only narrowly averted when the chemicals were banned. Then came Dutch elm disease; just as the birds began to recover, all the big elm trees died, taking away many of their favourite nesting holes. Owl boxes were the next step forward to help the owl and it looked as if recovery would again take place, but sadly hope has not been met by reality. The British Trust for Ornithology has reported a continued decline, with tawny owl numbers falling by 30% in the last eight years.

The continuing slide is being caused by the intensification of farming – destroying wild rodent habitat and therefore removing owl food. Local authorities must share the blame with their mania for tidiness, mowing and cutting every last square inch of roadside verge and suburban park, denying the owl anywhere to hunt. Tidy churchyards and sports fields are just as bad – and the curse of tidiness has spread to farmyards too – by order of our farming bureaucrats. Farmers are now obliged to keep birds (they are called vermin by the civil servants) out of farm buildings – therefore the barn owl is being denied its traditional nesting sites.

Fortunately all is not lost and the Countryside Restoration Trust has bucked the trend on its Lark Rise Farm in Cambridgeshire. All around our field edges we have grass margins, with a mixture of long grass and short grass; ideal habitat for voles and mice. We deliberately leave untidy corners and we have not 'tarted up' an old barn – it can be used by any wildlife wanting shelter. We have old spinneys and new spinneys and as a result we still have little owls and tawny owls and at harvest a short-eared owl was actually following the combine, hunting exposed mice. Better still we have put up barn owl boxes and five years ago – after a gap of forty years – truly wild barn owls returned and this year we had two successful broods: one in a barn owl box and one in an old willow tree. If only our political masters would come and see what can be done for all farmland wildlife with a mixture of care and common sense, the British Trust for Ornithology would then simply have to count the birds – not try to save them.

27

Happy Birthday Hunt Ban

———

Well, well, well – who would have thought it – the hunt ban is now a year old and virtually every hunt is still hunting – legally of course. They are hunting trails; they are flushing to birds of prey and they are just taking the hounds out for exercise – a giant sized, mounted 'walkies'. Of course some antis are aggrieved – they are shouting 'foul' and it is clear that many of them simply wanted to stop 'toffs' riding out in the country. Some antis are still turning up in some areas wearing balaclavas and carrying clubs and baseball bats; if I went to watch Cambridge United dressed so beautifully I would be arrested immediately, but assorted yobbos are allowed to wander through the countryside dressed like terrorists; 'the war against terrorism' evidently involves only some terrorists. To make matters worse antis are even blowing hunting horns and 'hollering' trying to lure hounds away from the huntsman to follow a real live fox. Although this clearly breaks various laws on 'incitement' I know of no hollering, horn-blowing, balaclava-wearing, baseball-bat-carrying countryside lover being asked to meet the local magistrates – why not?

In addition to my surprise at the hunts adapting so well to the new rules, the other surprise has been caused by the number of people attending. At one recent meet of my local hunt – the Cambridgeshire – it was just amazing – there must have been two hundred riders, as if people young and old, duke and dustman were making a point about bigotry and unjust law.

Some antis claim that the law is being broken and show great indignation. Why don't they show the same indignation against car drivers on their mobile phones and those cruising along motorways at ninety? Of course it is still to be tested whether Tony Blair broke the law during foot-and-mouth. Two Cardiff law professors think the breach of the law during the 'contiguous cull' was quite clear-cut – so why won't a Chief Constable from an old infected area, or the RSPCA, organise a prosecution to see if the law was broken? David Campbell and Robert Lee have written in their paper *The Power to Panic; The Animal Health Act 2002*: 'During the foot and mouth epidemic of 2001, the government engaged in *ultra vires* action on a huge scale, for it had no power to slaughter perhaps the majority of the 7 million animals it nevertheless did slaughter in the course of the 'contiguous cull''. They go on to describe what happened as 'executive contempt for the rule of law'. I have always thought that we were governed by the 'rule of law', not the manipulation of the law. In addition I was always led to believe that the law applied to everybody – me, Lulu and the Prime Minister.

I am glad to say that my bridesmaid is hunting well, within the law, and is thoroughly enjoying it. She greeted me like a long-lost friend the other day and I regret to say that I think her tongue actually went into my mouth. Yes, Corset the Cambridgeshire foxhound, which I 'walked' as a puppy and who accompanied me and Lulu down the aisle, is still fit and well. When I see her at a meet I only have to call her name and she charges at me often leaping up to head height. At the last meet she saw me first and nearly knocked me over – I can't wait for her retirement, when she comes to live with us and her big muddy feet will be padding all over the living room floor. Lulu is thinking of inventing elasticated paw pull-ons for the day that Corset approaches the front door directly from the cattle yard.

Of course many hunting antis simply don't know how important the hunts are in the social life of rural communities. The other day we decided to go to the Hunt Supporters supper – but lost the details under the huge pile of wood pulp that comes through my letterbox each week. I phoned a 'friend': 'Yes its black tie and starts at 7.30', he said. Despite hating dressing up I arrived looking like a corpulent penguin and it soon became clear that I was a genuine Jackass penguin. It was an informal supper and it started at 8.00 – even Lulu thought it was funny. I shall take my bridesmaid next time.

Hounds are not the only 'working' dogs that I meet during the winter as the CRT's tenant farmer has two little shoots at Lark Rise Farm with completely wild pheasants and Tim uses his spaniel as a 'retriever'. I attend as a beater – not wanting to shoot, but greatly enjoying roast pheasant, and twenty birds is considered to be a good day. This year we saw the best piece of retrieving ever. A pheasant was shot and fell to the ground – a fox rushed out, picked it up and disappeared into the undergrowth. A fox retrieving on a shoot – a politically incorrect fox – I wonder what the antis make of that?

28

One Man Without His Dog

After much thought I have just done something extremely stupid – I have renewed my TV licence. £126.50 gone for what? Cricket, that has disappeared, 'Match of the Day', (thank goodness Gary Lineker has at last stopped wearing a suit), 'Midsomer Murders' and 'Have I Got News for You'. The rest is sheer dross – Eastenders, countless make-over programmes, repeats of repeats, the unfunny Graham Norton, and yes, the new, dumbed down and dreadful version of 'One Man and His Dog' – no thank you very much – what a waste of time and money. The images of Springwatch were wonderful – but the inane waffle passing for commentary was what I would expect from somebody who lives in the middle of London – thank you and goodnight Bill Oddie – where's the 'Off' button? Oh for the good old programmes that could bring the 'On' button back into use? Where are the imaginative new programmes? And where is the real 'One Man and His Dog'?

I always loved 'One Man and His Dog' – it was good uncomplicated television-wallpaper; just the thing for a cold winter evening, requiring no thought or concentration but giving simple relaxation and enjoyment. To the hill farming community it gave recognition and opportunities during a very hard economic time and it gave urban Britain a chance to see and understand not only the best of rural Britain – but also the best of rural culture.

The invitation to put in for the job of 'presenter' for 'One Man and His Dog' came out of the blue. I had just contributed to a documentary about the countryside by the retiring 'Doggie' presenter, Phil Drabble, known also in disgruntled mood as 'Foul Dribble'. I had been looking at birds, butterflies and flowers with my old friend Gordon Beningfield and the producer had said: 'You must put in for 'One Man and His Dog', you are a natural'. Much to my amazement, and despite the fact that several top, established presenters were already on the short list, I got the job.

From 1994 until 1999 it was both a privilege and a pleasure to present the programme. I felt a close affinity with the shepherds and farmers who took part, and to this day I am intrigued and amazed at the relationship between man and Border collie. Having sheep myself and still living on the farm where I was born, I found it easy to mix with and talk to those taking part. There was plenty of good 'crack' both on and off screen, which helped put them at ease. Viewers from both town and country loved it.

Whispers started; the Controller of BBC 2 thought the programme was no longer suitable for modern, urban Britain. The programme was moved to 3.00pm on a Saturday afternoon, when even I didn't watch it. I said 'It's a ploy to reduce the viewing figures'. The faceless ones at the Television Centre said, 'It is a very good slot'. The Controller of BBC 2 at the time was one Mark Thompson, now Director General – he moved on to Channel Four. The new BBC 2 supremo was Jane Root; suddenly she said – surprise, surprise – 'the viewing figures are so low One Man and His Dog has got to go.' Was this 'Public service television' at its best, or a cynical manoeuvre?

With the help of *The Daily Telegraph* a campaign was launched and thousands of protest letters arrived at the *Telegraph* offices, which I then delivered personally, by the sackful, to the BBC – 'they' were not amused. As a result Jane Root announced that 'One Man and His Dog' would be spared and brought back in the form of a 'Christmas Special' – and behold dumbed-down 'One Man and His Dog' was born. The new producer informed me that sheepdog trialling on television was 'difficult for the general viewer to understand' (after twenty-four years) so changes had to be made – coloured team shirts had to be worn and celebrities introduced, oh dear – it was not just diabolical, it was embarrassing.

The 'crew' presented me with a beautiful engraved crook for saving the programme that they enjoyed helping to make; the Controller had other views and my presence on the programme was reduced until in 2001 I was told that I was no longer required 'because of your attitude towards the programme' – and, more worryingly, 'because of your other activities'; political correctness and the BBC's 'thought police' had struck. My crimes were apparently numerous – writing my book *The Hunting Gene*, speaking at countryside rallies and standing for Parliament as an anti-EU candidate – so much for free speech in Britain and so much for the BBC's own programme-makers guidelines – perhaps I ought to move to Iraq. By coincidence, since 2001 another little fat man has seen his BBC star rise; that is the year in which Bill Oddie became a Vice-President of the League Against Cruel Sports. Oddly, during the BBC's recent Anniversary Celebrations both Jane Root and Mark Thompson regretted the demise of 'One Man and His Dog'; it was fascinating – executive crocodile tears.

This year the BBC has announced not just a single 'Christmas Special' – but two whole programmes consisting of semi-finals, and the final. Bizarrely, England, Ireland and Scotland make up the semi-finals – Wales did not compete despite the fact that it was in Wales, at Bala, that the first sheepdog trial was held in 1873. The Welsh National Sheepdog trials were due to take place on the BBC's chosen filming day, and in typically arrogant BBC fashion, the Corporation would not change the date. The Welsh were not pleased; at the Denbigh Show an official of the Welsh Farmers Union said: 'What crap. It can't be a proper competition then, can it?'

When the Editor of *Weekend* asked me to visit the filming at Chatsworth House I readily accepted. 'We'll arrange for you to meet Ben Fogle', he informed me. 'Who?' I asked. 'The presenter – Ben Fogle.' I thought Ben Fogle was a place in 'Monarch of the Glen' (another BBC programme that started well and has since become unwatchable).

Ben Fogle was very affable and pleasant with a cut glass Bryanston accent. 'Where do you live, Ben?' I asked. 'London' he replied – sheepishly; perhaps one of The Archers ought to front Newsnight or the London Proms. To me his co-presenter looked like a cowgirl – a reincarnation of Doris Day – very strange. I suppose she was supposed to look like 'Fashionable country'. 'Quiet please', the floor manager shouted to presenters, competitors and crowd, 'broad smiles please – remember this is an entertainment programme.' Oh dear.

'It's awful', said one of the competitors afterwards, 'my friends love sheepdog trialling but they won't understand this.' With Lulu, my wife, we watched and listened. Cards were being drawn to decide competitors for each competition amid much backslapping and amazement. A spectator from Yorkshire said: 'I wish we could have the old programme back with you – this is rubbish.'

A few weeks before I had taken Lulu to see her first sheepdog trials at the Rydal Show in the heart of the Lake District. Hundreds of spectators including many holidaymakers were watching, and from their applause they seemed to understand the whole thing. As if to confirm this, every few minutes I was approached by total strangers to be asked: 'When are they going to bring back 'One Man and His Dog'?'

At Chatsworth Lulu said: 'Shall we go? – this is not nearly as good as Rydal – although that Ben Fogle is very fit.'

'Oi, that'll do Lulu – come by.'

29

Dressed to Kill

———

The phone rang: 'Oi Robin I saw that picture of you in the *Mail on Sunday* at London Fashion Week' – my head and chest were already swelling. I was proud of my appearance in the middle of all those bony models and preening fashion groupies. With my exciting mixture of farm clothes and natural scents I believe that I was already well ahead of the fashion game and well on the way to becoming an icon. Jimmy Hibbert went on: 'We think you could have done much better for yourself – we would like to change you from a walking haystack to man about town.' How dare a man who says 'Oi' tell me I look like a walking haystack? 'It will be a complete make-over', he went on, 'you won't just get a suit – you'll be given an image consultation; then you will have a facial, a wet shave (I have a wet shave twice a week anyway – clever Dick) and male grooming. (Male grooming? I didn't like the sound of that – surely that is what chimpanzees and orang-utans do?) Finally you will get a massage (a massage – my shoulders have never been right since I was tossed by one of my cows last year – yes – tossed by a cow –

not a funny experience) – then, with a glass of wine you will leave here feeling as if you can take on the world – it is a new way of buying clothes.'

I needed half an hour to think this through. I hate shopping – unlike Lulu. I hate new clothes – unlike Lulu. I want to go to the next Ashes Series – I don't want new clothes and an Aga – unlike Lulu. Anyway, what's wrong with wearing Y-fronts, odd socks, discarding my false teeth, only bathing on the longest day and the shortest and getting my sister to cut my hair four times a year? The cows and sheep think I look quite attractive – as do the free-range hens. Then there is the issue of travelling to London – I hate it at the best of times – but in the winter? Londoners may be frightened of bird flu, bumpkins like me are terrified of 'London travellers' flu' – with all colours and creeds coughing over you in the Underground, and then there is the issue of those breeding flu bugs in London's offices being transmitted to everybody on recycled air. Lulu was keen: 'Go on Pagey – do it – show me what I could have married.' Yes, she has started calling me 'Pagey' after watching the summer's cricket – Freddie, Warnie, Hoggy and so on.

'O.K.' I said, 'I'll do it – I've got a lunch date. I'll come up and be re-launched then.'

'Where's lunch?' Jimmy asked.

'Drones Club – Hanover Square', I said. That'll teach him – we old country boys may look like haystacks but we get around.

I arrived in London after being coughed and spluttered over for an hour and half. I was looking like a particularly flourishing haystack as I arrived at Waterloo. A shopfront proclaimed 'eel and Shamash'. 'How multicultural is that?' I asked myself. I had only seen 'eel and mash' in the East End before – 'eel and shamash' must be a mix of East End and Turkish. I took another look – no it wasn't 'eel'– it was a shopfront trashed; it should have read 'Steel and Shamash' solicitors.

The shopfront of 'Dress2kill' was very smart with the shop-girl in a well fitting striped suit. 'Would you like a glass of wine?' she asked – ushering me to a large leather sofa – was this shopping? 'What's it like being a shop-girl?' I asked in the aftermath of Cheri Blair's patronising and condescending remarks about shop-girls. 'Don't talk to me about that woman', Jelena replied. Perhaps Cherie should come to Dress2kill for a makeover – although what they would do with somebody who looks like a walking letterbox is quite beyond me. If only Cherie had worked in a shop she might have been good at her job and met and married a nice, honest young man.

Jimmy bounced in – a beefy, jovial rugby player who wants to create a club atmosphere for people buying clothes and bespoke suites. 'You go into a shop in Savile Row and its almost like going to church it's so solemn – we want you to enjoy it; have another glass of wine.' I needed it as Shirley Biggs the image consultant and fellow Director of Dress 2kill listed my fashion deficiencies. 'You look a mess', she said, 'you have a square-shaped face and with all that hair on top and side-whiskers you look bullet-headed.' Bullet-headed? 'Yes, bullet headed – you've got no forehead – you look as if you are trying to hide under that mop.'

'But I'm growing a pony tail!'

'Why?' she asked without sympathy. 'It will make you look fatter and shorter.'

'But I'm an old head banger at heart and heard Status Quo the other day – Francis Rossi's got a pony tail.'

'But he's twice as tall as you.'

'Have another glass of wine', insisted Jimmy as Shirley confirmed the fate of my hair. Then I was colour matched – to match my eyes, shortly-to-disappear hair and bumpkin cheeks. I went through the lot: 'light and dark', 'cool and warm' 'bright and muted'. It was decided that I needed something cool, muted and not too dark – in my language something from navy to hedgerow brown, or cowpat green. We chose a rather nice light navy material with modest stripes 'to give you height'. What was excellent was the fact that it did not come from China; the material came from British wool, woven in Huddersfield and created into a suit in Goole – not far from John Prescott's constituency. It has always struck me that John Prescott would have made an excellent MP for Goole.

Measurements were taken and Sunil, trained in Bombay, looked very professional with his pins and scissors. 'Oh', said Shirley, 'you will need a pink shirt.'

A pink shirt! My rustic credibility was being compromised. I needed another drink – I must go to Drones. I was looking forward to dinner (posh Londoners call it lunch). The only London club I had been to before had been Annabelle's – noted for its dog hairs around one particular little corner.

London is full of 'celebrities' quite unrecognised by me. In the Drones Club, Ben and Zac Goldsmith were approached by somebody wearing an open neck shirt and jeans. I thought I was the only one with a dispensation to be scruffy: 'Smarten yourself up – you're a disgrace', I told him. 'You know who that was?' Zac said. I hadn't a clue – apparently he was someone called Guy Ritchie who is apparently connected in some way to the Virgin Mary – I didn't quite understand.

Drones is a very good club serving English grown, quality, seasonal food. I had turnip and chicken soup followed by 'bangers and mash' – wonderful. Business was done: I agreed to try and supply Drones with joints of organic grey squirrel to provide excellent free-range white meat – while at the same time saving red squirrels by reducing the number of alien greys.

Back to Dress2kill via The Mall – complete with dozens of Chinese flags. Can somebody please explain why some Presidents with bad human rights records get bombed by Tony and George Junior while others – just as bad – get invited over to have tea and buns with the Queen?

Oh dear – it was time to be de-haired on the face and head. Maurice was from Burma, a country well versed in clearing rain forest – he was now supposed to clear-fell my head. There were hot towels, cold towels and a white liquid – I was told that it was something called moisturiser, not mayonnaise; then came the wet shave, complete with badger-hair brush and cut-throat razor. Cut-throat razor! I hoped he was more skilled with the razor than some of his countrymen with the chainsaw. All my lovely locks fell to the ground including my side-whiskers – what will Lulu hold on to now when we drive cross-country to check the sheep? The few strands left were combed back, almost bouffant style. Potion was applied to hold it in place – my hair hadn't felt so warm and sticky since my tame vixen of twenty-years ago had suddenly urinated on my head.

To reduce the stress level Maurice gave me a facial massage – Shiatsu – very relaxing, although at one time I thought there was a danger of a nosebleed. More lotions and a body massage with Lisa followed – what joy to get such manipulation in my shoulders – this really was the way to get a new suit. Finally she produced tweezers and plucked my eyebrows – I'll never be able to look my mates at The Hoops in the eyes again.

It was time for the fitting: 'Can I have another drink?' I didn't recognise the fat bloke in the mirror opposite with the same haircut that I had when I was seventeen. Since then I have gone with the 'haystack' – unchanged since before the

Beatles seemed to be copying me. The pink shirt arrived, black leather shoes and then the suit complete with silk tie. I felt comfortable – except the hair and my beloved side-whiskers – the suit was fine, the shirt almost acceptable and the tie very smart – perhaps I could return to Drones with no dispensation.

There was only one true test of success or failure – what would Lulu say? When I arrived home feeling like a fish out of water she was on the phone talking to 'Badger'. I walked in – she screamed long and loud: 'Badger! this isn't the man I married – he looks like a poof.' Oh well – I had enjoyed the day – and soon the squirrel casserole was on the table.

30

Climbing High – Boyo

So, almost a year to the day after climbing Kilimanjaro with the tobacco fuming Christopher Booker, I clambered almost nimbly to the top of Snowdon. The three peaks, Ben Nevis, Scafell Pike and Snowdon – 11,175 feet – had been conquered. I just hope that all those aches and wheezes result in some sponsorship money for the CRT's Turnastone Court Farm in Herefordshire.

I hadn't been to the top of Snowdon since I went in short trousers as a boy, in the train, with my parents. I still remember the cold of that cloud-enveloped top. It was memorable for another reason too; a knock on the door of our lodgings and the fateful news came that an uncle had been badly injured in an Isle of Man TT Race and was not expected to live. He was my mother's wild eldest brother, who died a few days later. It's good to see how the later genes have become so rational, gentle and well behaved.

My last visit to Snowdon was more recent when, much to the indignation of The National Trust, the CRT tried to buy Snowdon and we were within a whisker of succeeding. Using wonderful geographical skills the then CRT Director had cleverly arrived at Carmarthen railway station (instead of Carnarvon) and so I had to do all the bargaining and bidding myself, together with Nigel Griffiths, a Welsh CRT member from Swansea. The men with briefcases and suits did not seem too amused to have competition. We wanted to keep

Snowdon as a number of working farms, which people could visit; the National Trust seemed to want it as a rocky theme park, with added sheep. After signing an agreement to allow hunting to continue the National Trust won. The actor Anthony Hopkins led the fundraising, making much of his Welshness. Shortly afterwards he went to live in America.

Isn't it odd – when the sun is shining and there are butterflies to see or hills to climb, volunteers fall over themselves to check that there is no cheating; when the chill of autumn cools the air, climbing companions, including the excuse laden Booker, are very thin on the ground. To confirm that I climbed the last of the 'three peaks' I went with an old village-footballing veteran – Denis. We played football together for years. I retired at 48 – he played on until he was 53. I lost count of the number of times I had my name taken, or was sent off – usually for wanting to discuss in depth the referee's need for a white stick. Denis used to kick the opposition several feet into the air, but as he always helped

them up he never got booked – all except once. He was not actually playing, but a visiting unregistered player was booked for a foul and blurted out the name Denis Bishop – so Denis was booked for a foul when he was actually fifty miles away! Oh dear, football is corrupt from top to bottom.

We plodded up the Miners' Route; it was spectacular with the peaks, lakes and valleys bathed in sunlight and the sound of water mingling with the cool breeze and the distant call of ravens. In places the path was lost where thousands of feet had speeded up erosion. It always astonishes me – in Africa I expect to pay to enter a national park and in Tanzania I willingly paid to climb Kilimanjaro – but in Britain cash strapped charities and National Park authorities are expected to provide free facilities for visitors who could easily help pay for these beautiful but over-exploited places. I would have been happy to have paid £10 a time for Ben Nevis, Scafell and Snowdon and money is certainly required on all three to reduce the impact of so many weekend feet.

The view from the top was spectacular, but brief – the Isle of Man, distant Dumfries, Anglesey, Bardsey Island – wonderful – and then the cloud rolled in. It was packed at the summit – all those uncollected £10 – what a waste of potential conservation funding. Perhaps Margaret Beckett should put her caravan on the train so that she can see the possibilities. Avoiding the temptation of one-way tickets down, we plodded back down to the café by the car park to sample the worst beans on toast I have ever eaten – eaten on a crumbling polystyrene plate with a plastic knife and fork and with polystyrene tea. Perhaps at £10 a head Snowdonia National Park could invest in some china, cutlery and cookery lessons for the café staff too.

31

Old Granny

———

When I started keeping sheep about twenty years ago, a neighbour gave me some good advice. 'Robin', he said, 'remember, a good shepherd cannot afford to be sentimental – if you are it can be very costly in time, money and emotion.' It was such good advice that as usual I totally ignored it and as a result I have just paid the penalty in time, money and emotion. The simple fact is that Old Granny, my favourite toothless black sheep has just departed for that great sheepfold in the sky and the final decisions were difficult.

Her whole life was a drama. She started off as a result of a genuine ram raid. My neighbour's ugly Texel ram took a great shine to my beautiful Suffolk and Jacob ewes. He became so obsessed with their sultry ways that he simply walked through his sheep fencing and through my electric fencing too – without flinching from the blue sparks that shot from various parts of his anatomy. I then had to bundle him back – the difference being that I hate getting shocks from electric fences. One afternoon he was so desperate to get to them that he took off along the bottom of a ditch with me on his back. Having a fleece, he was quite unharmed by the experience, while I was almost shredded by the trailing brambles.

Finally, fearing for their good name I moved them – oh dear, it was too late. My girls usually lamb in April; suddenly, one ice-filled February night, three ewes lambed unexpectedly. Out of five lambs born on that bitter night only one survived – 'Granny' – a lovely black lamb with a distinctly Texel face. So right from the start there was sentiment; she was a favourite – a survivor.

She survived again several years later. I was just about to leave home for the filming of the last 'One Man and His Dog' before it was dumbed down so ridiculously. I was late and tempted to leave before checking the sheep, but – sense prevailed and I went to see them. It was lucky I did – the field was littered with dead and dying sheep and others had dreadful wounds. They had been savaged by stray dogs – somebody's pet: 'Oh Rover would never hurt a fly'. Granny was on her side in a pool of blood with a great lump ripped out of her throat. The vet came; we buried some, he treated others and he said that he could do nothing for Granny. He gave her some antibiotics just in case and again a miracle happened – against all the odds Granny survived.

With the passing of time her old wounds affected her; at times her breathing sounded worse than mine when I have bronchitis and she developed a touch of arthritis and lost some teeth; I should have sold her – but I kept her. What should I do? I felt I owed her a longer life – and yes, my judgement was ruled entirely by sentiment. Big Dave is one of several locals who help me on the farm from time to time and he is one of those unusual people who have a genuine gift for understanding and getting on with animals. Granny started losing weight: 'Let her lamb again', he said, 'it will keep her occupied – it will give her an interest.' She lambed again and looking after her daughter really did give he a new lease of life.

She did not like last winter and by the spring she had stiffened up. Should I put her down or keep her and let her lamb? The vet came again – more drugs including steroids – over a hundred pounds spent on an almost toothless old ewe, all skin and bones. She gave birth to another beautiful female lamb and she was transformed – mother and lamb did well. Half-way through the summer she left the main flock and came down to the yard – her lamb came with her before running back to the others to play. I fed her sheep nuts and each time she saw me she would 'Baa' an acknowledgement. Occasionally she would wander into the old orchard and try to graze with her one front tooth and molars. It was clear – a decision had to be made before another winter – a decision made harder by the Government's absurd and ridiculous regulations on 'fallen stock' – rules made only to hide their own inefficiencies and absurdities during foot and mouth. Now all animals that die on farms have to be carted off for incineration – emotion, sentimentality and common sense are no longer allowed on British farms.

The vet came – a good, understanding man who we regard as a friend. Her end came quickly and I found myself fighting back tears – tears for a sheep, for goodness sake. Oddly the rest of the sheep hung around the yard for several hours afterwards – entirely out of character, and they were back again the next morning. Now the farm is quiet and I still miss her greeting when I walk into the yard. And was she carted off in a lorry for incineration? I did what my conscience told me to do....

32

Hit Wicket

Where did the summer go? It simply flew by, helped, I suppose, by the fact that about thirty beautiful, exciting, breathless days were removed from reality, as I sat glued to the television set watching the cricket. 'Have you been to check the cattle yet?' 'The sheep?' 'The hay?' 'Have you started your new book? And have you written your Country Diary?' The answer was always the same: 'After the cricket.' And there was poor Lulu wanting to go and check up on Old Granny, our favourite toothless sheep, and to see, from the safety of the car, whether Alan, the ferocious Aberdeen Angus bull, had done his stuff. A fast bowler with the ferocity and build of Alan – what a frightening thought.

But the good news from all this is that Lulu, who comes from a cricketless background, has started to like cricket too. She now recognises 'Freddie', 'Gilesey' and 'Hoggy', and to keep in the jargon she calls me 'Pagey'. I must get a couple of name stickers for the car windscreen: 'Lulu' and 'Pagey' – almost as good as 'Kevin' and 'Tracey'.

She found my cricket gear quite confusing at first: 'I didn't know you had a motorbike'. 'No – that's a cricket helmet. That's a bat. That's an arm guard – those are batting gloves – and please don't touch that without wearing your Marigolds.' The good news from all this is the fact that at the age of sixty-two, I have not retired. This year, I didn't get picked once by the village team, but I have definitely not retired. They did ask me if I was available one weekend – but sadly I was judging carved sticks in the Lake District.

That is one of the good things about cricket, age is not important. There was an old rat-catcher in these parts a few years ago who played until he was eighty-two – he had to bat with a runner and field in the slips, but he and his team-mates loved it and he still boasted an almost perfect cover drive. Even now at the age of sixty seven my good friend, fellow European rebel and searcher for truth, Christopher Booker plays cricket enthusiastically – polishing the leather and waving the willow as if he is trying to swat some malevolent European Directive. Only recently he featured in a record last wicket stand of 57 for the village of Litton, in Somerset – what dedication is that?

I actually played in a team for the Countryside Restoration Trust that included Mr Booker, a few years ago. The game took place on a wonderful cricket ground on a farm at Bishop's Lydeard near Taunton. Sadly, the ground has disappeared; the state of dairy farming is so depressed that cows now graze the field as a matter of financial necessity. However, the farm is still close to cricket – outrageously, two Australians, Paul and Sally Bradbury, have been making their wonderful cricket bats in outbuildings for the whole of the summer. Some members of both the Australian and English teams use the bats – but they peel off the Bradbury label and put on the labels of their sponsors; in my opinion that definitely is not cricket.

The reason I have not been selected this year is simple – last year being tossed by the cow damaged my shoulders to such an extent that I could not bat or bowl in comfort, and so this year I have been happy that younger players have now

been found to replace several geriatric members of the club. That is the real joy from this cricketing year – teenagers again want to play. Children have even been seen playing spontaneous cricket on the village recreation ground with plastic wickets – a sight that has been absent for several years. Village cricket was dying on its feet – as we old codgers died on our feet – and this summer has seen a resurgence. It is a welcome resurgence, as cricket has been such a wonderful part of village life for generations. In almost every village in Cambridgeshire somebody will come up to me and say: 'I haven't seen you for years – do you remember the game when you ended up in hospital (ball hit eye)', 'I got you out' or 'you scored some runs.' One of my dashing shots even ended up being discussed at Lords. The bowler came up to bowl, the ball slipped out of his hands, and just before it trickled to second slip I rushed out and smashed it unsportingly for four. The questions were – was it a dead ball or was it a four? The answer was simple – it was in fact 'four wides', as the umpire had already signalled a wide.

My greatest innings was just as memorable. Second ball from a frisky young fast bowler; I was hit on the head – my helmet was undone and promptly fell on the stumps; that one was easy – out – hit wicket.

So I am grateful to Freddie, Gilesey and Hoggy for giving us all such a happy summer. To show my gratitude it looks like a trip to the Ashes series in Australia; sorry Lulu – I think the Aga will have to wait.

33

National Trust or National Mistrust?

Peter Rabbit and his friends don't know how lucky they are. If Beatrix Potter had invented Master Rabbit today he would be in big trouble. Gardener Mr McGregor would be on the verge of retirement, with the National Trust wanting to turn his vegetable patch into an up-market patio, leaving Peter Rabbit with no carrots to pinch; Mrs Tiggywinkle would have nowhere to hibernate as all the autumn leaves would be swept up for the sake of tidiness and Jemima Puddle-duck would have been left to the foxes long ago. But fortunately for generations of children Beatrix Potter wrote her wonderful stories before the Lake District was seen as a gentrified, homogenised, playground for second-homers and camper-van-drivers, when it was still a place where local people lived, worked and played.

To her the Lake District was far more than rabbits, mice and Squirrel Nutkin, for beyond her stories she saw a living, working countryside containing real people and communities, and with her money and her foresight she tried to keep that rural culture going. She loved the farms and their farmers; the small rural communities tucked away in spectacular valleys, and she loved the livestock of the fells.

The sheep that fascinated her more than any other was the Herdwick – now officially registered as a 'Rare Breed'. The Herdwick is an incredible breed – looking rather like a Teddy bear that eats grass. Its history is just as odd and shrouded in mystery; it is a real Lake District variety, with some stories suggesting that it came with the Vikings. The area reminded them so much of home that they decided to have their own Scandinavian sheep living with them. Another story claims that Herdwicks were on a Spanish galleon that sank off the coast of Westmorland – the animals struggled ashore and made the fells of the Lake District their permanent home.

The hill shepherds fascinated her too, and she loved talking to them, hearing their stories and appreciating their skills. In order to keep their way of life going she bought over 4,000 acres of some of Britain's most beautiful countryside, and she was concerned for the 14 farms, cottages and sheep that went with them.

Because of her wish to keep the farms going with their shepherds and their sheep, when she died in 1943 she left all her Lake District land to her husband and then to the National Trust, on condition that they 'let and manage the same, as far as possible, on the same lines as previously let and managed during the lifetime of myself and my said Husband'. Now, appallingly the National Trust is about to break that trust, and I write this as an embarrassed and concerned member of the National Trust's own ruling Council. Some members of the Council of course believe that decisions taken should be supported by all Council members under the banner of 'corporate responsibility'; sorry – I regard the National Trust's plan for High Yewdale Farm, in the heart of the Coniston and Little Langdale area of the Lakes, to be a prime example of corporate irresponsibility and dishonesty.

It is a beautiful farm – one of five farms together, all owned by the National Trust, and it is the only one making a profit from solely farming activities, with the others having to resort to B & B, holiday cottages and tea rooms to make ends meet. In 1985 it was selected as the ideal fell farm for the

Queen to visit and the tenant, Jonny Birkett, is still there. Sadly, at seventy-two, Jonny is about to retire, and astonishingly, the National Trust intends to divide up his land between the other farms and re-let the farm buildings for residential purposes. In other words, the wishes of Beatrix Potter, the donor, are to be ignored, and a profitable farm is to be broken up; the move has all the hallmarks of a land agent's plan executed to secure the National Trust more income. The message is simple – the hierarchy of the National Trust will ignore the wishes of a benefactor whenever and wherever it suits them.

What makes the plan worse is the fact that Jonny's father was actually head-hunted for the tenancy by Beatrix Potter herself: 'She came to see Father at least three times', he says, 'and chose him as she liked the look of him and he was a good shepherd. To me as a child she looked like a witch with long black clothes and clogs made from wood and leather with a metal buckle. Once we were at High Yewdale she came three or four times a year. It is a good farm, the best in the area. We never have to buy fodder not even in the winter and we have our own 'hefted' flock of Herdwick sheep – the same one that was here when Beatrix Potter bought it.'

A 'hefted' flock is a flock that that has the unique ability, passed down through successive generations, to graze in defined but unenclosed areas, known as 'hefts'. If the farm is changed, or the pattern of grazing is changed then this 'hefting' can also be broken. Sadly, Jonny's son is unable to take on the farm as his health has been damaged by organophosphate sheep dip, and so instead of being re-let, the farm is to be broken up. Despite a petition, the views of Coniston Parish Council and the efforts of the High Yewdale Farm Action Group, which includes vets, farmers and members of the public, the National Trust continues on its way without, it appears, the ability to listen or consult.

Eric Tailforth, a nearby National Trust tenant with his own hefted herd of Herdwicks, has no doubt that the National Trust's plans are wrong: 'I think the National Trust has made a decision and does not want to change its mind. If they carry on with what they have planned it will be a disaster for the farm and for the National Trust itself. You cannot justify splitting up a good farm for others.' Professor Sheila Crispin, a well-known vet, is equally irritated. 'It is a strange decision to take out the most viable farm with a hefted flock'. David Bolton, a farm business consultant of Andersons East, whose family has owned property in the Lakes for several generations is simply baffled. 'I would be surprised if land was the limiting factor here', he says, 'more likely the scarce element is marketing skill which could make an enormous contribution given the opportunities presenting themselves there. In general you would look to reinforce success and not reinforce those already in difficulty.'

The National Trust says that hill-farming is in crisis and the Government's ill-thought-out reforms of the Common Agricultural policy will make matters far worse. Peter Nixon, the Trust's Director of Conservation, says: 'Our hearts want to retain the farm, but our heads won't let us put in a new tenant to experience penury.'

Sadly, the National Trust is missing the point. With its land, membership and financial clout it should be showing the way forward for rural recovery, not meekly taking the easy option; it should be leading not following. As David Bellamy says: 'Surely the National Trust should be sticking to the spirit of Beatrix Potter's will and keeping the Lake District as a landscape of bite-sized working farms selling a diversity of locally produced food. With 18 million stay and 23 million day visitors using Wordsworth's Outdoor University every year, plus three million paid-up members, farm gate supplies, local outlets and an on-line catalogue could pay their way in a much more sustainable way. Peter Rabbit and Herdwick Sheep forever.'

Since 1999 I have been urging the National Trust to go further. It should be setting up its own food halls in places such as Ambleside, Keswick and Kendal. By selling its locally produced food, together with regional food, quality food, and low 'food miles' speciality products, not only would the National Trust help to keep its own tenants in business but it would also make far more money for itself than in breaking up farms and breaching trust.

Last Sunday I went to see the Duchess of Devonshire's farm shop at Chatsworth in the Peak District. It was heaving with people and in addition to her own produce she was selling 'Trent Valley Beef in Melton Red Ale', 'Sherwood Forest Pork in Honey and Ginger', 'Shackerdale Chicken Breast Escalopes', 'Cotswold Handmade Meringues', 'Orkney Herring', 'Somerset Cider Brandy' and 'The Gardeners' Tap', Chatsworth's own bottled ale – in effect the shop was a celebration of British food. It is the National Trust that should have set the lead in this sort of good food selling; for the sake of its Lake District tenants, for the memory of Beatrix Potter, and as an example to the rest of British farming, it should pull its complacent finger out.

34

Short Back and Sides

I am proud of my hair; I have never used 'Wash and Go' and very little of my hair has gone – oh, and if any Wash and Go's solicitors are reading this chapter in this age of litigation, I had better explain that this is an unfounded little joke. Sad times we are living through!

Having a full head of hair has two main advantages; first it keeps the ears warm during winter and second, when I speak to groups of farmers I can use it as a visual aid. 'Look at my hair', I tell them, 'this is how your hedges should be – wild, with plenty of cover for wildlife to nest in or seek shelter. Cut it when it needs a cut – I cut my hair every three months, if it needs it; cut your hedges every three years, but only if they need it'.

Oh dear, then came a telephone call from somewhere called London – *The Daily Telegraph* wanted a new picture of me and would I get my hair cut. Oh dear, oh dear. What a time to ask, just when the National Hedge Laying Championships were about to be held in the village; how those hedge layers would laugh as they were trimming the hedges. In addition I had a harvest supper to speak at and prizes to give out at a

Farming and Conservation night in Suffolk. I tried to delay things. With low country-cunning I said 'Yes, if you pay', believing there would be a rapid retreat – I have not paid to have my hair cut since visiting the Rhodesian War in 1976. There a very camp but pleasant old gentleman, who today would be driving a pink Land Rover Freelander, cut my hair in a cellar below the famous Meikles Hotel – it cost me a dollar – £1. 'Oh that's fine', came the immediate reply, 'come and have it cut at The Gentry at Canary Wharf'.

Twenty-eight pounds later I emerged, cold, and not recognising the fat bald figure following me as a reflection in the shop windows. After twenty-seven years I realised that I had still got ears; but £28? What an experience; I have not yet recovered from the attack with the hairdrier – a hairdrier! My farmyard credibility is in tatters. A backward-leaning hair wash too; it was like being christened and more frightening than when I was dunked in a cage to see a Great White shark.

Then of course Badger Walker arrived, my old hedge-laying friend who was to compete in the 'National'. I can still hear his peals of laughter as he said: 'Did they give you the needle or did you have gas?'

At the harvest supper – more laughter. I urged them all to visit the National Hedge Laying Championships. 'Egg-Laying Championships?' one old girl asked. I advised her to have her hair cut, it would help her hearing. Badger, a sad Manchester United supporter, had a wonderful evening; he sat next to a Manchester United supporter who travels all the way to Old Trafford every fortnight from Ipswich – they never stopped talking. Badger continued training until one in the morning on my Bramble Whisky – it is a good job that hedge layers don't get urine tested.

The Championship took place on a farm at the other end of the village – Badger was feeling confident. I had asked the officials to visit the CRT's Lark Rise Farm to cut our hedges

– but they saw my neighbour's and went there. Frankly I think hedge laying next to our six-foot deep ditch would have added to the spectacle.

Incredibly, during the course of the day some of the hedge layers were regaled by a middle-aged lady who said: 'How dare you destroy these hedges – it's vandalism – they will all die.' One of the major arts of hedge laying of course is to keep the hedges alive and to give them more vigour. At the end of the day the hedges looked wonderful, almost as tidy as me with the hedge layers using as much skill as my hairdresser, but without the hairdryer. The sad news is that Badger only came fifth in his class; the good news is that Manchester United lost at home.

35

Up Your Kilt

Before my bosom friends in the Gloucestershire Constabulary start jumping up and down and shouting: 'Racist, racist', as they appear trained to do, let me say straight away that this chapter is not racist or anti-Scots – how can it be when I am indeed part Scot. It is not a very large part, but it is an historical fact that in the dim and distant past ancestors of mine were captured by the Roundheads at the Battle of Dunbar and then marched down to the English Fens. As far as my history recalls, all this excitement in the family happened in about 1600. Why my relations were captured in the dead of night is anybody's guess; perhaps they had forgotten to go to bed in their kilts; too much porridge for supper – who knows? All we know is that they ended up in the region of what is now the Ouse Washes and an obsessed Dutchmen put them on the end of shovels, which is where they spent their days – shovelling fen mud and with hundreds of others turning the Welney area into one of the most amazing drainage systems the world has ever seen. Astonishingly, one of my Scottish relations now runs his cattle on summer grazing created by those prisoners of war, having travelled a historical journey from felon to farmer. The prisoners themselves, of course, suffering from bad backs and the 'fen ague', became delirious and fell in love with fen women – hence the arrival of yet more of my Morton relations into the Fens.

The other day I made the return journey to the Highlands and there I was in the dead of night, under a starlit sky sitting in what I believe is Scotland's greatest contribution to the cultural life of the planet – a 'hot tub'. In the middle of winter we had done the sauna – inhaling scalding steam to damage the lining of our lungs; jumped into the plunge pool – a real, icy mountain stream collected in a concrete sided puddle and then into the hot tub. What is this modern fad of sitting in hot tubs really about? A hot tub is simply hot bubbling water. I suppose again my ancestors would have sat in a large puddle and numerous 'old wifies' would have been slaving over a hot fire topping up the hot water. And where did the bubbles come from? with a diet of porridge and whisky perhaps it is not hard to imagine – or perhaps a tame herbivore, a sheep or a calf, joined them in the hot puddle.

Believe it or not New Zealand has even more bizarre politicians than we have and their farmers are now actually taxed on the greenhouse gases produced by their sheep and cattle. Sadly this is true, causing New Zealand farmers to form an organisation called Farmers Against Ridiculous Taxes, known as FART. Perhaps we should start a similar one – Farmers Against Red Tape.

Scottish bliss – so I am told – the hot tub, plus a wee dram. That is probably how my ancestors were taken at the Battle of Dunbar; they were sitting in a hot puddle, drinking whisky instead of defending themselves. But even whisky is over-rated; in the main it looks like hillside run-off and tastes like hillside run-off, but this year I have found a way of making whisky drinkable. Buy three bottles of the cheapest whisky possible; add a quarter of a bottle of black rum, a pound of blackberries and a pound of sugar. Swill it round the jar every few days and drink when the last of the sugar has finally dissolved – what a drink. Even this has been eclipsed by good old-fashioned English drinks. This year sloes have hung on the blackthorn like grapes and the quality of the sloe gin is absolutely wonderful; but there is an even better drink – the elixir of all drinks, and needless to say it is not Scottish – it is quince gin. Take four pints of diced quince (discard the cores); add four pounds of sugar; put in a one gallon jar and cover with about 2 and a half pints of gin (preferably export). Shake every day for three months and then taste the pure, pleasurable golden ambrosia.

This Christmas morning as my Scottish friends are enjoying themselves sitting in their bubbling imitation puddles and sipping their alcoholic run-off, I shall be sitting in front of a log fire with a mince pie in one hand and a glass of quince gin in the other; that is of course until there is a knock on the door – no it will not be the Jehovah's Witnesses, it will be: 'Good morning; I am from the Gloucestershire Constabulary; I understand you have written an inflammatory article about Scotsmen.'

36

Stands the Church Clock at Ten to Four?

———

Doesn't time fly when you're enjoying yourself. After so many years of enjoyable bachelorhood I have now been in a state of matrimonial bliss for over a year – and when I say bliss I really do mean it. It is astonishing how time flies and after my regulation bath on the shortest day we celebrated our anniversary at the Rupert Brooke in Grantchester, where we had our reception twelve months earlier. Obviously the shortest day is a popular date for promises and of course Elton John followed our example. Oddly we have had a couple of gay ganders on the farm for a number of years, it is true. It is also the first time I can remember such a long-term unorthodox relationship among our farm animals. With this politically correct government in power it can only be a matter of time before they can legally marry too. I wonder what a marriage between gay ganders would be called – a goosing? If we have a goosing here, who wants to be bridesmaid?

Sadly in one year the Rupert Brooke has changed; it has been tarted up and has moved from being a village pub with a restaurant, to a restaurant with a wine bar. This whole area of Cambridgeshire is being homogenised and sanitised, as a pocket of 'rural' England becomes 'suburban' England. The food was excellent, but the bar area once used by the locals with their pints has gone, tidied up. I suspect that the pub is now an establishment that Rupert Brooke would not have felt happy visiting. According to the oral tradition of the village, Rupert Brooke went to the pub to enjoy the company of the locals – the farm workers, the horse keepers and the shepherds. Now to enjoy the company of genuine locals he would have to move down the road to the Blue Ball, and there would not be one farm worker among them. I wonder what he would have made of the present residents of the Old Vicarage? (Mr and Mrs Jeffrey Archer of course.)

Sadly the suburbanisation of South Cambridgeshire has recently been demonstrated in a most outrageous way. South Cambridgeshire District Council, on which I have served for over 36 years, (and which has surely become one of the worst local authorities in the country) has just banned a local resident from keeping cockerels and a few ducks and geese in his large garden. All this after just one complaint (from a couple wanting to sell their house) and in spite of a petition wanting the rustic noises to remain. To fight the Council the couple would have needed over £7,000 – an amount they could not afford. Apparently this is known as 'the rule of law' and 'British justice'.

> Stands the church clock at ten to four?
> And isn't the Council such a bore.

After our wedding proper we had a wonderful party for those friends we could squeeze into the local horse arena. There young and old all became born-again groupies of The Wurzels, still drinking up their 'zider' and proclaiming the wonders of combine harvesters after all these years. These old ravers were such a success that we are having a re-run, when the weather gets warmer, although why wait for the weather to get warmer – they, and we, are all getting Bomber Blair's 'heating allowance' anyway.

The Rupert Brooke is not the only place to have been

tarted up as Page Pastures continues to sparkle under Lulu's magic touch. Not only does the living room carpet remain visible, but the bedroom carpet has now appeared too. At the same time I have remained reasonably healthy during this winter – the first almost bronchitis-free winter for years – I wonder if it is because all the dust has gone. The sound of the Hoover also appears to have driven out the mice that usually take up winter residence in the cottage. Gone are the days when I would wake up in the middle of the night with a mouse sitting on my head – yes it really did happen.

One day Lulu brought something odd into the house. At first I thought it was a surfboard – but she can't swim. Apparently it is something called an 'ironing board'; for those wanting to indulge in this pastime I am told it can be made more exciting and done for sponsorship. As a result 'extreme

ironing' has taken place on the top of cars, mountains and even under water; I think I will leave that to somebody else.

There is just one crisis in our marriage at the moment – I must confess. I only have to leave a piece of clothing on the floor – where I always used to leave it – and Lulu scavenges it immediately and washes it. At the same time she is a brilliant cook and feeds me well. This means that as my clothes shrink my waistline expands. But even in this there is a good side. The most abused and ill used food in modern Britain is gravy. Most disgusting, thin liquids called 'gravy' are disgraceful apologies for the real thing. Lulu makes wonderful, thick, steaming, succulent gravy. I have only known one woman make it better and that was my late mother – what greater compliment could there be for a new, happy life and wife.

37

Beware of Stoats

If the winter be cold and bare
Travel about with extra care.
Beware the hunting of the stoat
For he'll grab you by the throat

According to some old country stories we should forget bird flu and the wild boar that have recently become very wild in Devon, our main worry at this time of year should be stoats. That's right – stoats. Apparently, a cold winter can make stoats form packs – the ferocious little animals then hunt together and sometimes, when conditions are right, they will attack people. So be warned, all those stockbrokers who have bought old farmhouses at the edge of woodland in Surrey, or who have a holiday cottage in Norfolk; if the night is clear and cold and you hear a strange murmuring and chattering coming towards you, get inside and slam the door – it could be a stoat attack. That is the story – but is it true? I have lived in the country all my life and have been in isolated places at all times of the day and night and have been attacked by nothing – apart from a stroppy Aberdeen Angus bull and an over-protective cow with its calf. In addition I have had many encounters with stoats and have lived to tell the tale – they have all been frightened by me.

James Wentworth Day was a country writer who did as much as anybody to spread the story of fear and havoc caused by stoats – and he was very good at exactly that – stories. He was a competent naturalist and a fine writer, but on occasions his imagination, and his pen ran out of control.   It is true that stoats can be brave and relentless hunters but most hunting animals are aware that they must avoid injury and are very careful when attacking animals much larger than themselves. The largest creature I have heard of attacked by a stoat was a heron. Alas, after early success the heron shook the stoat from its neck, speared it with its beak and swallowed it head first for tea; it was a long meal as an adult stoat is about a foot long, together with a four-inch tail.

The only cold weather fact that can be confirmed about the stoat is that in the northern parts of Europe stoats turn snow-white in winter, as camouflage, except for the conspicuous black tip to the tail; hence the rhyme:

> *An animal I know is very forlorn,*
> *It's cursed by all gamekeepers as being base born.*
> *They trap it, and shoot it, and say it is vermin,*
> *Then flog it to royalty who wear it as ermine.*

I have only ever seen one 'ermine' stoat in Britain and that was in the Brecklands of Suffolk.

There is no doubt that the stoat is a remarkable animal; it is in the weasel family (Mustelidae) and is a cousin of the weasel, polecat, pine marten, badger, otter and mink. Some people see a flash of brown streak across the road and ask, 'Was that a weasel or a stoat?' The answer is simple:

> *The weasel is weasilly distinguished*
> *But the stoat is stoatally different.*

In simple terms the weasel is a third of the size of the stoat and the stoat has a long tail with a very prominent bushy black tip. This tail can be very useful means of defence if the stoat is attacked by a bird of prey.

The stoat's reputation is not helped by its hunting habits – it hunts by day as well as night. It eats nuts and fruit, as well as birds, fledglings and eggs and will also tuck away the odd frog and toad, but its favourite meal is rabbit – which is also the most accessible. One rabbit will be selected and it will be hunted ruthlessly by scent, all other rabbits being totally ignored. Finally, when the rabbit is exhausted, the stoat will strike and often the rabbit will scream as it dies – a sight and sound that most non-country people brought up on a diet of Walt Disney's Bambi and Mickey Mouse find quite shocking. Then the stoat will suck the blood of the rabbit it has just killed. Oddly, the old gamekeepers would steal the rabbit from the stoat if they could, as a bled rabbit with no lead shot in it made an excellent dinner.

So the stoat is often seen as a bloodthirsty savage animal, whereas the fox, which is just as ferocious, is universally loved as it performs most of its dirty deeds after dark. Typically in *The Wind in the Willows* the stoats and weasels were depicted as nasty bullying brigands invading Toad Hall from the Wild Wood. As far as I am aware there is only one story praising stoats: *Hunters of Longtree – A Cotswold Tale*. It is the stoat equivalent of *Watership Down*, but sadly for the author David Walker, despite being a very good book, stoats don't have the same appeal as bright eyed cuddly rabbits.

There is one common misconception today. It is often suggested that gamekeepers, to protect pheasants, persecute stoats. In facts stoats were trapped and killed long before game shooting became popular. In those days back garden hens were important to village people for both meat and eggs and so foxes and stoats have been killed to protect domestic poultry for hundreds of years.

The breeding habits of the stoat are odd. Some scientists claim that the male mates with his daughters while they are still in the nest. Then an odd biological quirk, 'delayed implantation', (a phenomenon shared with badgers and roe deer) means that they do not actually become pregnant until later in the year. The mother will give birth to between five and twelve kits, or kittens, in the spring and she is a very good mother. Once the family leaves the nest the young will follow her, and later they will help her to hunt. An old Norfolk gamekeeper has seen this several times in late summer. 'Sometimes you can here them coming', he says, 'there will be a murmuring – mmm mmmm mmmm mmm – as they all keep in touch with each other and they will be very tightly grouped. If you startle the mother she will spit and scold you.' Consequently his view is that the 'pack' is in fact a family, with some of the young males being even larger than their mother.

David Walker, while researching his book, came across three incidents of attacks, all mentioned in *The Field* magazine and he believes that in each case it was a mother with her tribe of young. On December 2nd 1922 a woman in Cornwall reported that a stoat from a pack attacked her shoe and then her bicycle tyre. In September 1920 a woman in Perthshire suddenly had one hanging onto her skirt, which she simply shook off and in June 1923 near Burton, a man going for a walk had an angry stoat try to climb his leg and the gang of gibbering, muttering stoats followed him half a mile along the road. So it seems that many of the tales are simply of parents defending their young.

But there is still one more tale reported in *Country Life* of a woman in Surrey in the early 1950s returning home from the farm dairy on a bitterly cold January evening: 'It was not dark, thanks to the starlight reflecting on the snow. I had gone past the ash tree at the crossroads when I heard a shrilling noise, a chittering of many tiny voices. I stopped and looked towards the wood and saw a shadow emerge from it about 70 yards away and move over the snow towards me. I ran back to the ash tree knowing I had to get up it somehow. I had never climbed it before, but, driven by desperation, I scrambled up into a V of branches and watched a wave of stoats break against the trunk. There could have been 50 of them swarming around it, eyes glowing, for what must have been ten minutes, but which seemed like hours. I was alternately praying and cursing. Then they must have heard something, because one of them gave a sharp commanding call. All the others immediately packed behind it and swarmed through the hedge on the other side of the lane. From my vantage point, I could see them move over the adjoining field. When they were out of sight, I collapsed out of my tree and ran all the way home'.

So, who knows? Just in case, I will continue to carry my trusty stick, whatever the weather.

38

Feather-bed or Subsidy?

I have just celebrated receiving my third Winter Fuel Allowance. I had intended putting the money towards a trip to Barbados to see the cricket: 'Barbados', I thought, 'that should keep me warm enough', but alas, there is so much to do here and so many battles to fight that I have decided to stay at home. Instead I went to have a medical, to see if I will last another sixty years. Oh dear, that was a mistake; another sixty days and I will be lucky. The trouble is that I have matured from being 'mildly obese', to 'fat'; fortunately the rather nice doctor and nurse were far too polite to put any other word before or after 'fat'. The other worrying point to emerge is the fact that the height of a normal person is supposed to be twice the waist measurement; you are reading the words of someone who should be 7ft 2ins, but who in reality lives life at a much lower altitude.

I write all this to emphasize the fact that just because I have reached a certain age I am now being subsidised. Although I am fit and hope to last more than sixty days I am getting a heating subsidy, a rail fare subsidy and a health subsidy in the form of free prescriptions, although I do not really need them as my circumstances are exactly the same as when I was fifty-nine and received nothing. But I am not alone; my young niece receives a generous weekly subsidy in the form of child benefit – what I still call 'family allowance'. This subsidy has always amazed me; how can

147

we in the First World actually give money to people as a reward for breeding, when we continually harangue the Third World for having high birth rates? To make matters worse, we are even more densely populated than India and China, but in a politically correct country we are not supposed to raise matters like this.

Then look at the lives of our MPs; the whole of their generous salaries and expenses come directly from us – a 100% subsidy courtesy of the taxpayer. I have been a District Councillor for over thirty-five years. When I started we got nothing, it was considered to be 'public service'; now we get paid an inflated monthly allowance and some of my colleagues claim extra expenses as if it was Christmas – computers, mileage allowances, and so on. 'Public service'? Sadly I think it has become 'troughing' from the public purse. Is there anybody reading this still unsubsidised? If so, where do you buy your food? Do you buy oranges? Do you buy Chilean asparagus in December or American plums in Tesco's during our own plum season? If you do then you are indirectly subsidised too. With no taxes on aviation fuel you are buying subsidised food, which means that your life is being subsidised.

Thanks to political lightweights such as Bomber Blair, it is the political fashion at the moment to criticise farm subsidies. Like 92% of the farming community I would be very happy to receive no farm subsidies; but the facts are simple. Firstly I believe more than ever in the wisdom of 'food security'; that a country such as Britain should produce as much food as it can in a responsible way. Despite those who preach 'globalisation, globalisation and yet more global-isation' we live in a very insecure world with climate change, terrorism, aggressive regimes and politicians kept in power through the weapons of mass deception; consequently such potential instability means that 'food security' is a matter of common sense and good housekeeping. If that common sense requires subsidies to maintain good food production – so be it.

In addition to this, most people want a system of environmentally friendly farming to cover the land to produce barn owls, skylarks and cowslips as well as wheat, beef and eggs. To achieve this, farming cannot be totally 'efficient' as chunks of land have to be left looking 'inefficient'. I do not believe that this should be a matter of choice, but a matter of responsibility – we have a responsibility to look after our land, our landscapes and our wildlife as we produce food. Then of course there is the matter of food quality itself. How can British farming compete with cheap Third World farming? The globalisation apologists have been telling us for years that imported food is produced to the same high standards as in Britain. After seeing on the news the way poultry are reared and treated in Thailand, during the Avian flu epidemic, all I can say is 'pull the other one, it's got bells on'. Yes, to stand any chance against that sort of food production, we need subsidies.

I cannot understand why British politicians and consumers have got a fixation on 'cheap food'; why can't we be like the French and appreciate good, quality food. Most of the people I know haven't got clapped out Lada cars; they haven't got lino on the floor; nearly all of them have electrical gadgets in their living rooms and kitchens that they do not really need – so why is it only food that comes down to cheapness? If the good old British shopper was prepared to be more discerning and pay the proper price for farm produce there would be no need for subsidies. Sadly the good old British shopper does not pay a fair price for food – and why not. Stand up the SUPERMARKETS with their famous 'armlock' – but that is another story. Until that arm-lock is broken, responsible farming means subsidies.

39

Happy Birthday BSE

———

It is a strange state of affairs. Recently, we have seen anniversaries for two major agricultural disasters, and now various scientists, and branches of the media, seem to be willing us into another high profile farming fiasco. Incredibly it is over ten years since BSE was linked with variant CJD creating a food and health scare of astonishing proportions; this was followed five years later by foot-and-mouth disease. Now some of the same scientists who ordered the obscene cull of livestock during that catastrophe have twitching trigger fingers as they anticipate the arrival of bird flu.

The BSE debacle was a scandal in its own right, when hysteria overtook both logic and science: it was claimed that there was a link between BSE in cattle and variant CJD in people, although I have yet to see any evidence that confirmed the theory. The media went wild – *The Observer* newspaper predicted a million dead by 2016 and the Government's top BSE scientist thought that deaths would reach half a million, in a plague that would be 'worse than AIDS'. Christopher Booker of *The Sunday Telegraph* was like a voice crying in the wilderness when he said it was scaremongering, that there was no proven link between BSE and CJD and that the slaughtering and burning policy for old cattle was ridiculous. Having wasted £4 billion on slaughtering healthy cattle, the total number of CJD cases is still only 150 – and rather than escalating out of control it has, fortunately, almost disappeared.

Some scientists are still crying 'Wolf! Wolf!' of course – in their desire for research grants; but the only thing clear about BSE and CJD is that scaremongering took place on a massive scale. I believe that BSE was caused by organophosphate chemicals being used on cattle – affecting their central nervous systems – while at the same time new Euro-rules allowed rubbish meat waste to be fed to herbivores. To embarrass the old Tory Government a Public Inquiry was held into BSE as soon as Labour was elected – but it came up with no sensible conclusions; putting the blame on Europe or DEFRA (more accurately, DEATHRA) would have opened up claims for compensation on a massive scale.

Every cattle farmer in Britain was hit by BSE. Normally I have my livestock killed as close to the farm as possible; it is humanely produced meat. Sadly, my old cows have had to be carted long distances to a special slaughterhouse and incinerator in the Midlands because of BSE rules. They have been mixed with cattle from other herds and carted miles along motorways – against my wishes, but there was nothing I could do about it.

Foot-and-mouth was a similar farce. The big difference between foot-and-mouth and BSE has been the fact that the Government refuses to have a proper public inquiry into foot-and-mouth – presumably because its policies created such a shambles. In addition there are various aspects of the outbreak that the politicians do not want placed in the arena of public debate. I, and the Countryside Restoration Trust, supported vaccination from day one. It has been used successfully in other countries and I simply do not understand the objections to it in Britain. In addition I do not believe the tale that the virus arrived in swill fed to pigs in Northumberland. Sorry, there are simply too many convincing alternatives. There are a variety of stories which claim that foot-and-mouth was rampant in sheep in Wales long before it was discovered in Northumberland. There are also some very responsible people who believe that the whole tragedy resulted from a government-run live-virus experiment that went wrong. That is the particular version I believe and there are individuals who appear to have convincing evidence.

It has to be said too, that the 'contiguous cull', involving the slaughter of 7 million healthy animals was almost certainly illegal; a fact confirmed by two Cardiff law professors. In November 2003 I reported to readers of *The Countryman* that I had complained to the Chief Constable of Gloucestershire on behalf of a farmer who had seen his livestock illegally killed. Predictably the Chief Constable refused to take action – claiming legal advice to support his inaction: astonishingly in this age of 'freedom of information' and 'data protection' the Chief Constable then refused to let me see his advice. Consequently, with no prosecutions from apparently widespread Governmental law-breaking, it is difficult to decide whether we live under 'the rule of law' or 'the political manipulation of the law'.

And now of course we come to bird flu – I have written to DEATHRA's Secretary of State, asking for permission to vaccinate my few free-range hens; I think if I send the Labour Party fifty quid I have more chance of becoming a member of the House of Lords.

40

What a Wheeze

Lulu woke me up at two o'clock the other morning: 'Listen', she said, 'there's a flock of geese flying over the house – listen to them calling.' Geese at two o'clock in the morning? Most of the thousands of wintering geese in Norfolk had already left for their breeding grounds much further North and in any case we live in Cambridgeshire, not Norfolk. We listened again – geese? The noise certainly sounded like geese but it was actually coming from inside the bed – we listened again. Oh no – the squeaks and whistles were coming from my congested lungs, for the second time of the winter. Lulu apologised for waking me and was soon back snoring (that is huge exaggeration but it sounds good after being woken up that early) but I could not get back to sleep. I was worried in case a mutant virus miraculously jumped from me to the birds in my garden giving them human flu, and causing a pandemic that could wipe out millions. Then of course I worried in case animal rights activists started campaigning to have all human flu victims put down to save our bird population; with the Government being so close to various animal rights groups and after pocketing hundreds of thousands of pounds from them over the years, this could be a distinct possibility.

My concern with all the metropolitan media scare-mongering about bird flu is for the welfare of my free-range hens. I have just written to Mrs Beckett wanting permission to vaccinate my hens against bird flu – I assume she won't let

153

me of course. The Vietnamese can, the French can, but the British Government appears to love killing farm livestock – they have even changed the Animal Health Bill so that the slaughtering illegalities that went on during foot-and-mouth are now legal. In any case it is illegal to kill a badger or a sparrowhawk – but fine to wipe out farm livestock. It is all right for me to vaccinate my ewes against various diseases, but not all right for me to vaccinate my hens. Surely this indicates Mad Minister Disease?

It is bizarre too – the nanny state of New Labour has been urging people to eat better food – organic and free-range eggs being part of the mantra. Now all those farms that have responded and gone free range are the ones who will see their hens immediately slaughtered in the event of a bird flu outbreak. 'All hens must go inside' will be the order, 'or they

will be slaughtered.' The large producers will simply not have enough buildings to put all the birds inside and they will be culled. Several of those officials involved in the foot and mouth fiasco are being lined up for the bird flu response – déjà vu – welcome bird flu. Livestock control, environmental health and agricultural red tape must be one of the biggest job creation schemes ever thought up by this government; the bureaucratic cocktail at last answers this question: Why did the chicken cross the road? Answer: To create fifteen jobs, thirteen forms, six European directives, four Ministry booklets and employment for two Spanish vets, neither of whom can speak English.

My hens will be all right in theory, they are true free-range and go where they like, when they like and even walk into my sister's farmhouse when the door is open. Of course DEFRA, or in this case, 'DEATHRA', has insisted that all flocks of over fifty have to register – more control and red tape. Fortunately the local foxes have put my flock total down to 45 and so I have been spared yet more regulation.

The scare stories about bird flu have been remarkable. It seems to me that the BBC – the Barmy Birdscare Corporation – actually can't wait for bird flu to arrive. The other morning after speaking at the Chester Business Club I watched BBC Breakfast Time on the hotel's television. What a relief I don't normally watch it. Still, there it was, in February, with the presenter suggesting that swallows would soon be returning and they could bring bird flu; and presumably if they fly low enough they can watch Breakfast Television. Instead of saying 'what nonsense' the representative of the RSPB and a female BBC wildlife presenter took the inane, scaremongering questions seriously – they were to wildlife behaviour what Tessa Jowell is to Mortgage Awareness. Now, when the swallows arrive – usually around here in late April, I suppose there will be people demanding to knock their nests down, along with those of house martins – well done the BBC.

Animal scares have got well and truly out of hand in this urban dominated society. When Tilly and Alan Smith took their Cairngorm reindeer to Pickering, before Christmas, the local council absurdly bought 20,000 wet wipes in case people touched the reindeer. Afterwards Tilly was not amused: 'From the state of some of the onlookers', she said, 'we needed to wash down the reindeer after being in contact with people – not the other way round.'

41

How Old is my Brain?

———

'Oi Robin' (it was that man again) 'will you go to London for us and play a new computer game?' 'What?' I couldn't believe my ears – I rarely 'do' London and I certainly do not 'do' computer games – ever. I have watched nieces and nephews glued to screens for hours on end like Zombies from another planet – and do not want to join them in their transfixed state – no thank you very much. My refusal actually made me feel quite smug; with two billion video games sold worldwide – I do not own one of them and have no wish to own one of them. In addition, of the 350 million hardware units sold globally, not one has entered my life – Game Boy, Donkey Kong, The Legend of Zelda – who are they? What are they? I haven't a clue and I don't want to know.

Yes, I have a mobile phone with computer games on it; I have no idea how to play them. The other day when the phone seized up an eight-year-old got it going for me again. Yes, I also have a computer, this article was written on it. But when I bought it it took me an hour and half to get it out of the box and another hour to switch it on – that's how IT literate I have become in this golden age of 21st century electronic junk – designed in Japan and packaged in Beijing.

On the day I was invited to London my computer doctor told me that as far as he was concerned the only virus that was not attached to my machine's innermost organs was for bird flu. To unscramble the electronic constipation he used something called a 'Panda'. I thought Pandas hung about trees sucking bamboo – sorry – but that's the stage I've reached; apparently not – this Panda navigates the highways and byways of my computer's interiors, munching unwelcome viruses.

Oh, but there was more – there always is. A sting in the tail – the ultimate humiliation – call it what you like: 'We know you don't like London and we know you don't like computer games – but there's a new game out developed by a Japanese neuroscientist called Dr Ryuta Kawashima; it is aimed specifically at the over-45s and designed to stave off the onset of dementia'. The only word the nice *Mail on Sunday* man did not use was Alzheimer's – I suppose he couldn't remember how to spell it. Look – I know I'm 63 – I know its all downhill from here on – but I found it all rather hurtful. Had my lovely wife Lulu been speaking out of turn? I know I can never find my teeth – or keep them in; I know the other day I put my mug of tea in the fridge and started to drink from the milk jug; but surely that is not dementia? I know that I do have great problems putting names to faces and faces to names – 'Good to see you Robin – I haven't seen you since the Royal Show' – 'Who was that Lulu? I've never seen him before in my life.' Then of course there are my car keys. 'Where are they?' is a daily refrain. However, in my view, underpants are the real testers for dementia; the question is, how often do you put your underpants on back to front in the course of a year – or even a week? With me at the moment it is twice a year.

OK, so perhaps there was a case for doing a brain test – but again why me? There are many other over-45s who clearly need their brains sharpened up and from their inability to recall simple incidents and events they could be on the road to dementia much faster than me. Take Tony Blair for instance – the poor man is still looking for weapons of mass

destruction – he knows they were left somewhere, but he simply cannot remember where. John Prescott completely forgot about his Council Tax; almost certainly on the due date for payment he had put his underpants on the wrong way round. Then there was dear old Tessa Jowell – she appeared to have a complete blank on her mortgage repayment details, while John Reid, when Defence Secretary, suddenly failed to understand the simple phrase 'Civil War'. Worse still, Ruth Kelly, when Education Secretary, seemed to have had great trouble remembering all the details of her expenses and she is under 45 years old. So with all this happening to the brains of our political leaders – perhaps I should set the example and go and have my brain trained. If I can do it successfully, perhaps the great and the confused will follow.

We are, apparently, all living longer, and the longer we live so the brain dims – the lights slowly go out – we use them less and less until they cease to work. Good old Dr Kawashima believes that the answer lies in brain exercises. If we use the brain and exercise it the lights will remain plugged in, switched on and shining brightly. Just as jogging, aerobics and a brisk twenty-minute walk will keep the body exercised and healthy – so the brain also needs regular and repetitive exercise. The Japanese have taken to Brain Training as enthusiastically as they have to eating rice and killing whales. Launched in Japan in May 2005 *Dr Kawashima's Brain Training: How Old is your Brain* has already sold nearly 1.8 million copies and is still top of the software charts. Sales peaked on Japanese Respect-for-Senior-Citizens Day; in Britain such a day would be celebrated with unprecedented levels of pension and handbag snatchings.

Nintendo has already announced a £2m advertising campaign for the British launch of 'Brain Training' with *Saga Magazine* readers being a specific target; oh dear, I hope demand does not exceed supply – we must not have muggings and Zimmer frame attacks in old peoples homes as unruly Saga-louts search out the elusive Brain Age consoles.

So, with the help of my geriatric rail card I arrived in London to be one of the first people in Britain to have my brain exercised by Dr Kawashima. The Nintendo console opens like a book. The first challenge, how to switch it on, was totally beyond me – I had to be shown. On the left screen appeared Dr Kawashima, on the right screen – information – the wrong information; the date was wrong and therefore the information was wrong. Surely Dr Kawashima was the one needing 'Brain Training'? Or from the way he was behaving, dog training: – 'sit' 'quiet'. The electronics did not like being corrected. 'The game is closed down – goodbye.'

With help the Doctor came back – an irritating man accompanied by a never-ending stream of syrupy canned music coming from the box. With his jaw forever moving and balloons of useless information: 'this game activates your prefrontal cortex' and 'your belly needs food doesn't it? Well, so does your brain, and breakfast is key. A morning meal helps your brain run better – the brain needs carbohydrates.' What my brain didn't need was a little yellow man talking psycho waffle above a background of 'muzak'. The first game – with words and colours – came on: – the colour red, the word 'black' and I had to give the actual colour – repeated in various combinations and sequences; apparently speed being the key to brain age. This was followed by reading aloud – a piece from Jane Austen featuring, appropriately, a man called 'Pratt' – with the number of syllables per second being recorded. Each game was measured according to speed – 'walking', 'running' or 'cycling' – but no Zimmering. Then came adding, subtracting and multiplication, and then, dramatically: 'From the score we have your Brain Age'. This was it – how old was my brain? – 62 or what? 'Three – two –

one; your brain age is 80'. Oh, thanks a lot – I go all the way to London to be insulted by an electronic machine featuring a yellow man with verbal diarrhoea. Yes I know I couldn't find my teeth as usual but a brain age of 80?

The good news the electronic Doctor tells me is that with a host of further games and tests, including a never-ending supply of sudoku, and by using the built-in calendar – my performances can be recorded and my brain age monitored. I can exercise my brain and see the years roll away; clearly a good sales pitch for the ageing, commuting middle classes.

OK. I took the doctor at his word and play resumed – moving numbers of different colours – how many blue? Which is the highest number? The lowest? Order of ascent and descent – the only thing missing from the Christmas cracker puzzles was the Christmas cracker joke – or was that Dr Kawashima? After another thirty minutes of 'brain exercising' it was time to re-test my 'Brain Age': 'three – two – one 57'. So from 80 years old to 57 in thirty minutes – another two days of this and I would be re-developing acne. And did my brain feel exercised? – it did. How much would the game sell for? £19.99. What sort of people would buy this? Not me. Would it simply become a passing fashion accessory for commuters bored out of their heads as they went to work? Would geriatric Nintendo consoles take over from Bingo and Beetle Drives at 'The Over Sixties'? And, most importantly of all, if Dr Kawashima made a donation to Labour Party funds would he be made the first electronic Japanese peer to sit in the House of Lords? Yes – Dr Kawashima's Brain Training certainly exercised my brain – but it will never take my time or my money. It just seems extraordinary to me that with dementia – I'm sorry – what was I writing about?

42

The DEFRA Dawn Chorus

———

It is that time of year again when I fall out of bed well after lark rise – at about six – and fall in again around midnight, unless there are midwifery demands with a lambing ewe or calving cow. Lulu likes being married to a farmer and to make things even better she can stay in bed in the early morning when I am staggering into my Wellington boots – life is so unfair.

It has been a dry spring and the cattle are out of the yard and calving in the brook meadows where they find it easier to behave like wild animals. To be honest, the early morning journey to check them is not a hardship. Once, the dawn chorus had practically died, but now it is almost back to its full complement, with lark song, chiffchaffs and great tits 'saw sharpeners', so called because of their brittle, double-edged song. Soon, blackcaps and willow warblers, and hopefully the cuckoo will join them – although for two summers the parish has been cuckooless.

The cows pay little attention to my early visits; it is a peaceful time with a woodpecker drumming, a fox returning to its earth and woodpigeons clattering out of the old hedge. I hope ear-tagging the calves remains peaceful this year. After last year's head-butt battering, my shoulders are still not quite right. To prevent a repeat performance we have changed the system; we are not attempting to catch the calves in the open field; we are driving mothers and calves back to the farm where the stroppy matrons will be separated from their young by a large metal gate when the tagging is in progress. It is remarkable – farming must be the only profession in which Ministry red tape and regulation seem to over-ride the demands of 'health and safety'.

Ear-tagging, 'passports', movement records, all for cattle are nonsense anyway; they amount to red tape designed to deflect attention away from government incompetence, which was the real cause of the foot-and-mouth crisis. It is absurd; at the moment cattle are monitored more closely in Britain than asylum seekers, Irish travellers and dusky men with beards, carrying violin cases – how cowist is that?

In addition to checking my animals I have been hunting regularly over the past few weeks – breaking the hunting ban. With Lulu's three dogs, we have been hunting for frogs, bumblebees and butterflies. The questions are, do Henry, Harvey and Alfie constitute a pack, and does butterfly hunting with dogs break the law?

The first brimstone, flying on March 18th, immediately tried to commit hara-kiri by flying into a spider's web. I

rescued it – I rescued beauty from the beast. I suppose all those purists at the RSPB who claim that predators should be allowed to predate will say that I am becoming sentimental. I should have watched the brimstone sucked dry half an hour after waking from hibernation, as gleefully as the conservationally correct watch magpies scoffing the young in a goldfinch's nest and a sparrowhawk eating a song thrush alive.

Strangely, another unusual species has also been roused by the onset of spring – 'the shiny-shoed red tape flounderer'. Members of the pack usually arrive wearing smiles, glasses, shiny leather shoes and carrying bags full of forms. The first was from the County Council's 'Trading Standards' department – yes trading standards. He wanted to check the ear tag numbers of the cows, as well as the animal movement and drug books. He seemed happy. It seems only a matter of time before any sheep or cow that gets out without an animal movement form will have to be electronically tagged and trained to sign a form in triplicate. Why Trading Standards have to visit my cows and not DEFRA – the Department for the Elimination of Farming and Rural Affairs – is a mystery.

Next came a phone call from DEFRA's Animal Health Division. Did I feed my animals with supplementary food? Well yes – my cows and sheep have a few high protein nuts in winter, and my hens have 'layers pellets' all the year.

'Could I come and take samples?' he asked.

'Why?'

'Government regulations.'

'Why don't you visit my suppliers – Central Wool Growers at Bury St Edmunds?'

'I'm not allowed to, I have to visit your farm.'

'And where will you be coming from?'

'Bury St Edmunds.'

Oh dear – bonkers or what? And why couldn't the DEFRA 'shiny-shoed red tape flounderer' do the trading standards job at the same time? Please don't tell me – write to the Government's agricultural Red-Tape Queen, Margaret Beckett: am I suffering from failing vision or does Mrs Beckett wear a gas mask?

43

Single Farm Chaos

Do Bob and Tony read my books? That is the question. When I write Bob and Tony I mean of course those great humanitarians Bob Geldof, the Boom Town Rat, and our leader Bomber Blair. I want them to explain to me exactly what they mean by 'make poverty history'. The reason I ask is simple – at the moment British farmers are receiving £72 a ton for milling wheat (bread wheat), and if I understand Bob and Tony correctly British farmers are considered to be rich. Not as rich as New Zealand farmers, it would seem, who are currently getting £110 per ton.

So how are farmers in the Developing World getting on? Well, the going rate in Kenya for a ton of Kenyan grown wheat at the moment is a mere £151 – no wonder wheat is looking increasingly attractive to the Masai, many of whom now think that combine harvesters charging across the plains are a far better financial proposition than migrating wildebeest. This also explains why wheat fields are forming an ever-tightening noose around the Masai Mara Game Reserve – a fact not mentioned in the BBC's spectacularly self-indulgent and superficial series 'Planet Earth'.

So people whose incomes do not depend on the world

market, such as accountants, solicitors, pop singers and prime ministers, tell farmers they should not get subsidies, they should become 'more efficient' as they trade on the world market; yet most people in the world seem to be getting better prices than British farmers. There are even more interesting facts available. Where does British milling wheat go once it has been harvested? The obvious answer is in bread, cereals and biscuits. So from a packet of wheat breakfast cereal costing £1.50 – how much does the farmer get for his wheat? Answer – 5.25p. So where does the other £1.44 go? If wheat was making £90 per ton – a figure that would do away with the need for subsidy (the dreaded Single Farm Payment) the amount to the farmer per packet would be 6.75p – so who is making and taking the money?

Similarly if a 400gram loaf of bread was all wheat flour – at 70p a loaf, just 2.88p would go to the farmer. At £90 a ton the lucky farmer would get 3.6p per loaf – please don't spend it all at once. But how many loaves are 100% wheat? I recently bought a Kingsmill Wholemeal loaf. The packet informed me '100% wholegrain' and '100% taste', whatever that means. Yet in the ingredients panel it had only '61% wholegrain wheatflour', and it included 'soya flour'. I don't eat soya, as I don't want to aid the destruction of Brazil's forests, so I phoned Allied Bakeries, makers of Kingsmill Wholemeal Bread. 'Yes', I was assured, 'it's all wholegrain – including the soya'. 'But soya is a bean not a grain', I said helpfully, 'so how can it be 100% wholegrain?'

Tales from livestock farmers are just as bad and go to show why British farmers need their new all in one subsidy – the Single Farm Payment (SFP). The money most of them are getting for their produce is simply not enough to live on. I would rather the supermarkets paid a fair price for their food, but sadly in Britain there is no longer a 'free market', just a few monopoly buyers. Until a proper market returns we will all have to depend on our subsidies; but the next question to Bob and Tony as they 'make poverty history' is, where is our Single Farm Payment? It was promised in early March, but still has not turned up. The Scots and Welsh have received theirs – in England there is just a mass of red tape and delay and as a result many farmers have a choice – go broke or increase your borrowing.

The SFP as chosen by Mrs Beckett is the most complicated system of administering CAP money in Europe. Friends completed all my DEFRA forms, as I did not understand a word of them. Astonishingly too, the payments are based on land ownership in the years 2000, 2001 and 2002. This means that there are people no longer farming, who do not even live in England or own land, who will receive money. How barmy is that? Some time ago the Countryside Restoration Trust bought some land from Cambridgeshire County Council – incredibly the County Council will now get the SFP and not the CRT's tenant, Tim Scott, who needs it. Elsewhere, because Tim has taken about 30 acres out of production as a contribution to wildlife friendly farming, he has been penalised on those 30 acres and will receive no SFP. Those prairie farmers who cultivate every square inch of their land – right up to the edges of hedges and streams etc, will get the full amount.

The money was promised, according to DEFRA's own newspaper *Farm Link*, in early March. Because of the chaos the Head of the Rural Payments Agency has been suspended. The average farm income is just £16,000 per year – the overall head of farming in Britain receives a salary of £131,000 plus expenses of £69,757 and has just been promoted to Foreign Secretary. She has three residences and of course a caravan. Surely, after this shambles Margaret Beckett, the Caravan Queen, should not have been promoted; she should have been sacked.

THE COUNTRYSIDE RESTORATION TRUST

If you have enjoyed this book and would like to join the fight for the countryside through the CRT, write for details from:

The Countryside Restoration Trust,
Barton, Cambridgeshire CB3 7AG